Praise For Energize to Impact

"Charles told me about energy in business back in 2016. You need it, your team needs it, and any successful business needs it. The good news is that you don't have to wait until the end of the book. You will be energized with the flip of the first page!"

Soheil Chavoshi
Executive Director, ACADIA

"The author has mined his vast experience to make the case that an energizing and impactful leader must 'create and manage energy to drive change,' and he does so in an engaging and applicable format. He captures the humanity that is part of leadership, with examples that ring true to anyone working in a cross-functional business environment. Energize to Impact is both an enjoyable read and a useful guidebook."

Lefa E. Alksne
Director Research Program Management – Operations, Regeneron Pharmaceuticals

---

"The values and insight Charles provides in this book will raise your effectiveness, improve your performance, and create transformative and energetic teams to drive success, no matter the position, level, or industry. A truly special book that will energize you on how to impact for sustainable and successful leadership."

Lauren T. Dam
M.S. in Biotechnology Program, Georgetown University Medical Center

"An insightful and accessible guide for leaders who really want to deliver high-energy leadership that results in long-lasting benefits. Through a mix of case studies and open debate, the reader experiences the levers to understand how impactful leadership can be achieved and maintained. A must read."

Gordon Vater

Business Development Director Gallagher Bassett International

---

"The book's pertinence and didactic quality illustrate Mr. Dormer's expertise and passion for helping leaders becoming more successful. It speaks to all leaders at any rung of the ladder.

With each talking point being pertinent, everyone will find something valuable and worthwhile to take away.

If you are looking for a detailed road map to effective leadership, I highly recommend this one."

Chrys Esseau-Thomas

Division Coordinator at International Monetary Fund

"A blueprint for energetic, impactful effective leadership that is comprehensive. The four major sections in the book cover foundational elements and nuances of being a great leader. I especially appreciate the self-assessments and gap analyses, which direct the reader to personal strengths and potential weaknesses."

Kirk P. Walters

Principal, The Walters Group, LLC.

"A prompt for new leadership thinking. COVID-19 catapulted the business world into one that demands innovation and creativity. It is a blueprint for leadership at every level in the organization. The action plans serve not only as a great review of the concepts in the chapters but also a prompt for new thinking for any energized leader."

Kay W. Palmer

Founder, The 42 Group, LLC

"This book allowed me to understand where I currently was versus where I wanted to be, enabling me to analyze the gap so that I can accurately develop the strategy that is best fit to take me along the journey to ultimately achieve my purpose in life."

Christopher Steven Carlson

M.S. in Biotechnology Program, Georgetown University Medical Center

ENERGIZE TO IMPACT

Reframe Leadership for
Sustainable Success

ENERGIZE TO IMPACT

Reframe Leadership for Sustainable Success

Charles S. Dormer

Energize to Impact: Reframe Leadership for Sustainable Success

Copyright © 2020. Charles S. Dormer. All rights reserved.

Published by The DP Group, LLC.

ISBN: 978-1-949513-21-9

No part of this publication may be reproduced, stored in a retrieval system, or transmitted in any form or by any means, electronic, mechanical, photocopying, recording, scanning, or otherwise, except as permitted under Section 107 or 108 of the 1976 United States Copyright Act, without either the prior written permission of the publisher or author. Requests to the author for permission should be addressed to Charles S. Dormer, APEXEnergizingImpact@gmail.com.

Limit of Liability / Disclaimer of Warranty: While the author and publisher used their best efforts in preparing this book, they make no representations or warranties with respect to merchantability or fitness for a particular purpose. No warranty may be created or extended. Neither the author nor publisher shall be liable for any loss of profit or any other commercial damages, including but not limited to special, incidental, consequential, or other damages.

For my wife Trish and our family for their
energy, inspiration, and support

Acknowledgments

This book is a result of my leadership journey spanning almost forty-five years of my professional career. During that time, I had the opportunity to work with some great leaders. I am indebted to them for giving me the chance to learn how to be an energizing, impactful leader. These include Tony Chaplin, Dr. Gwyn Morgan, Dr. William Kerns, Dr. Robert Ruffolo, Dr. Paul Blake, Dr. Mene Pangalos, Dr. Frank Walsh, Dr. Giora Feuerstein, Dr. Amber Salzman, Dr. Ian Hau, Dr. Evan Loh, Dr. John Dent, Dr. Dennis Langer, Tom Mercer, and Dr. Matt Bell.

I created this book over the past six years and wish to thank all the people who helped in its development and bringing it to reality. I thank the following people who reviewed the book: Kirk Walters, Kay Palmer, Gordon Vater, Dr. Soheil Chavoshi, Dr. Lefa Alksne, Lauren Dam, Charlotte Vater, Amelia Dormer, Steve (Chris) Carlson, and Chry Esseau.

I wish to thank the faculty at the University of Pennsylvania, Dynamics of Organizations, who expanded my thinking during my time studying how organizations work, particularly Dr. Jean-Marc Choukroun, Dr. John Eldred, and Dr. Foulie Psalidas-Perlmutter.

I am indebted to the faculty and students at Georgetown University, Biotechnology Program, where it was my honor to teach for the last few years. I thank Dr. James Hawkins and Vasna Nontanovan for their support and the opportunity to pursue my passion. The journey to help young scientists prepare for leadership roles is still one of my great passions. I am particularly grateful to Dr. Jack G. Chirikjian, the founder of the Biotechnology Program, whose foresight and vision brought this program to life and gave me the opportunity to get involved. Although no longer with us, he is still an inspiration and one of the greatest leaders I have known.

I owe a debt of gratitude to numerous leaders whom I have coached. For confidentiality reasons, I will not name them here, but they know who they are. I learned more from them than they learned from me. I thank Ros Taylor, who inspired me to be a coach and taught me so much about coaching. Also, I thank all the great coaches I had the chance to work with over the recent years. They are always open to share their wisdom and experience.

Thanks to Divya Parekh and her team, particularly the lead editor, Kathleen, who worked hard to make my ideas accessible and clear. They are great publishing professionals.

Finally, I thank my wife Trish for her insights, support, and encouragement. This book would not exist without her. I also thank my children and their partners, Amelia, Charlotte, Christopher, Thomas, Gordon, and Bori, who inspired me, gave me energy, and were never shy to give constructive feedback. They continue to amaze me every day.

Table of Contents

FOREWORD	1
INTRODUCTION: FRAMEWORK AND FOCUS	3
Structure of this Book	4
CHAPTER 1: EMBRACING ENERGIZING, IMPACTFUL LEADERSHIP	9
Definition of an Energizing, Impactful Leader	10
Risk of Failure to Deliver	10
Integrated Framework for Energizing, Impactful Leadership	11
Challenges That Cause Leaders to Fall Behind	12
CHAPTER 2: UNDERSTANDING YOUR PURPOSE AND VISION: STRATEGIC THINKING	15
What is Strategic Thinking?	16
Levels of Strategy	17
The Importance of Purpose	19
Developing Strategic Goals	22
Initial Steps in Strategic Planning	23
Energizing, Impactful Leadership in Action: Purpose and Vision	25
Chapter Summary	28
Key Learnings About Strategic Thinking	28
Action Plan for Improving Strategic Thinking	30
CHAPTER 3: DEVELOPING STRATEGIC GOALS IN CONTEXT: SYSTEM THINKING	31
Understanding Your Organization	33
Changing System Elements	41
A System-Thinking Approach to Strategic Planning	42
Energizing, Impactful Leadership in Action: Putting Strategic Goals in Context	45

Chapter Summary	50
Key Learnings about System Thinking	51
Action Plan for Improving System Thinking	52
CHAPTER 4: EXPLORING SELF-WISDOM: INNER IMAGE	**53**
Why Self-Reflection is So Crucial to Success	54
Outcome Goals for Self-Reflection	54
The Impact of Self-Awareness	59
The Critical Skill of Having Empathy	61
How Your Mindset Affects Your Success as a Leader	67
Energizing, Impactful Leadership in Action: Developing Self-Wisdom	72
Chapter Summary	76
Key Learnings About Self-Wisdom	76
Action Plan for Developing Self-Wisdom	78
CHAPTER 5: SIGNALING TO OTHERS: POSITIVE PRESENCE	**79**
Positive Presence Component: Content of Your Communications	80
Positive Presence Component: Visibility	84
Positive Presence Component: Leadership Behaviors and Skills	85
Distractions From Being Present in the Moment	91
Mindfulness and Being Present in the Moment	96
Skills and Behaviors for Effective Listening	97
Skills and Behaviors for Influencing Others and for Power Dynamics	101
Energizing, Impactful Leadership in Action: Ensuring Positive Presence	104
Chapter Summary	108

Key Learnings About Having a Positive Presence	109
Action Plan for Having a Positive Presence	110

CHAPTER 6: CREATING A POSITIVE ENVIRONMENT — 111

Characteristics of a Positive Environment	112
Three Factors that Impact Creation of a Positive Environment	114
Be Intentional in Leading in a Virtual Environment	119
Energizing, Impactful Leadership Action Plan: Creating a Positive Environment	125
Chapter Summary	128
Key Learnings About Creating a Positive Environment	128
Action Plan for Improving Your Ability to Create a Positive Environment	129

CHAPTER 7: ENSURING EFFECTIVE DECISION-MAKING — 131

Stages and Consequences of Actions	132
What is Effective Decision-Making?	133
Selecting the Decision-Maker(s)	136
The Impact of Emotions in Making a Decision	138
The Impact of Biases in Making a Decision	140
How to Avoid the Influence of Emotions and Biases in Decision-Making	145
How to Avoid Emotions and Biases in Group Decision-Making	148
Energizing, Impactful Leadership in Action: Effective Decision-Making	151
Chapter Summary	157
Key Learnings about Effective Decision-Making	157

Action Plan for Improving in Effective Decision-Making — 158

CHAPTER 8: NEGOTIATING CONFLICT AND LEADING CHANGE — 159

Raising Conflict — 160
Negotiating and Resolving Conflict — 162
Energizing, Impactful Leadership and Negotiating Conflict — 166
Leading Change — 168
Energizing, Impactful Leadership in Action: Negotiating Conflict and Leading Change — 176
Chapter Summary — 181
Key Learnings About Raising and Negotiating Conflict — 181
Key Learnings About Leading Change — 182
Action Plan for Improving Negotiating Conflict and Leading Change — 183

CHAPTER 9: LEADING TRANSCENDENT TEAMS — 185

Setting Clear Purpose and Goals in Context — 188
Team Formation — 190
Team Conversation — 193
Team Development — 195
Team Decision-Making — 198
Energizing, Impactful Leadership in Action: Building a Transcendent Team — 201
Chapter Summary — 206
Key Learnings for Leading Transcendent Teams — 206
Action Plan for Becoming Effective in Leading Transcendent Teams — 208

CHAPTER 10: OPTIMIZING COLLABORATIONS — 209

Challenges of Co-creative, De-centralized, Complex Alliances — 211
Alliance Leadership in Practice — 215

Task and Delivery Factors	215
Trust and Relationship Factors	219
Assessing Partnering Effectiveness in Alliances	222
Energizing, Impactful Leadership in Action: Building a Transformational Alliance	224
Chapter Summary	230
Key Learnings for Leading Collaborative Alliances	232
Action Plan for Improving Capability to Lead in Collaborative Alliances	233

CHAPTER 11: CREATING ENERGY TO DRIVE CHANGE: DELIVERING AS AN ENERGIZING, IMPACTFUL LEADER — 235

Energizing, Impactful Leadership	238
Outcomes of Leaders Not Creating Energy	240
Journey to Becoming an Energizing, Impactful Leader	241
Integrating Key Learnings on How to Become an Energizing, Impactful Leader	242
Element #1: Strategy in Context	242
Element #2: Self-Wisdom	243
Element #3: Signaling to Others	244
Element #4: Understanding and Implementing Actions	245
Summarizing Your Leadership Impact	248
Simplify Your Journey to Becoming an Energizing, Impactful Leader	249
Your Journey Plan	249

Foreword

Why did I write this book? It grew out of three passions that drove my professional and leadership journey. The first was my passion for science and cellular pathology. I still remember looking through a microscope for the first time and viewing the wonders of the world of cells and organ systems. The different cell types still fascinate me. Why? Because they come together in an organ to perform the tasks needed for human life. But cells also can become dysfunctional and cause problems that result in diseases such as cancer.

Cellular dysfunction ties into my second passion: studying organizations as systems. Organizations are human systems that have many separate functions that need to work together. But, sometimes, there is dysfunction. The result is pathology that can derail an organization's mission.

Pursuing my first two passions, cellular pathology, and organizational dynamics, I studied elements (cells or people) that work together to form functional or dysfunctional systems. In organizational dynamics, I learned that systems are only as good as the leadership of individuals in the system.

My third passion is coaching leaders, helping them become more effective by changing their behavior. I witnessed firsthand the value of coaches in impacting a leader's behaviors and performance that result in the maximum impact on a system as a whole. Recognizing the importance of developing great leaders, I decided just over five years ago to work with individuals as an executive coach to help develop their leadership skills. This book draws upon the lessons I learned during my career.

Introduction: Framework and Focus

"We must all drive ourselves to the utmost limit of our strength. We must preserve and refine our sense of proportion. We must strive to combine the virtues of wisdom and of daring. We must move forward together, united and inexorable."

Prime Minister Winston Churchill
(Speech at Edinburgh, Scotland, October 12, 1942)

No matter your job title, if you are competent in your field but want to drive a greater impact through your work, this book is for you. If you want to become a strategic leader and influence others through collaboration rather than authoritarian behavior, this book is your road map. If you have an interest in rewiring your leadership capabilities so that you can be an energizing, impactful leader who delivers desired outcomes, this book will show you how to succeed.

People who want to become more effective leaders often face the same initial challenges. Does one of the following scenarios describe your situation?

- You need to take on more responsibility in your current role. You feel fear or anxiety.
- You need to transition into a new role with new challenges. You are overwhelmed or uncertain about the path forward and want to feel more in control.
- You need to be more effective at engaging with others and motivating them. You struggle with how to create energy among other employees to deliver the result the organization needs.
- You need to understand not only how to build momentum in

the business teams you lead but also how to sustain it.
- You were told that you need to work on your executive presence to get to the next level.
- You feel powerless or even depressed. Or you suffer from "leadership imposter syndrome."
- You are risk averse or even defensive about your behaviors. You are reluctant to go through emotional, mindset, and behavioral changes.
- You have limited time for learning how to become a more effective leader. Moreover, the number of books, articles, training programs, and coaches available overwhelms you. You want to determine what will enable you to make the biggest impact in the shortest time, but you are paralyzed as to what approach to use and stuck on knowing what to use as "first steps."

Highly effective leaders succeed not only because of what they do but also because of how they do it. Measuring leadership success looks at two dimensions: (1) delivering on strategic goals and actions for the leader's areas of responsibility, and (2) the impact of the leadership.

Energizing, impactful leaders succeed by developing a clear, compelling strategic vision and motivating others to follow that vision. They know how to create and manage energy in an organization to drive change and deliver the desired strategic outcome. They know how to create positive energy and minimize the impact of negative energy.

Structure of this Book

The journey to becoming an energizing, impactful leader is complex. Balancing the elements (or strengths) of effective leadership is a complex process. As with any complex journey, a simple road map is invaluable. This book is your road map. It will simplify your journey by showing you how to balance the complexities of leadership. And it will help you chart your course and track where you are in relation to achieving your leadership goals.

Action Plans. The examples of action plans at the end of each chapter present scenarios that leaders faced and detail the actions they took to improve their leadership capabilities. I changed the names of people and companies in these action plan examples to protect confidentiality.

Chapter Summaries and Key Learnings. At the end of Chapters 2-10 are summaries and lists of the key learnings. The endings of these chapters continue the action plans with self-assessment questions that will help you identify your strengths and your opportunities for growth as a leader.

Framework. Becoming an energizing and impactful leader requires having strengths in four interrelated elements. I refer to these elements as the Integrated Framework for Energizing, Impactful Leadership. This framework is a holistic, system approach to understanding leadership and its short-term and long-term challenges.

It is not possible to be an effective leader if you lack even one of the four elements. Thus, this framework presents crucial information you need on your journey. Chapter 1 explains the framework, and subsequent chapters focus on different aspects of the four interrelated elements.

Focus. Many books and articles on how to become a more effective leader present the information in a set of steps and the necessary sequence of those steps. In contrast, I recognize that leaders' initial scenarios and needs vary (as I described above), and you may first want advice specific to your current situation more than a set of sequenced steps to follow.

The first eight chapters of this book are stand-alone discussions of one piece of the overall integrated framework. You can choose to read them in the order shown in the Table of Contents or start in a particular chapter that meets your immediate need. For instance, perhaps starting with Chapter 4, focusing on self-wisdom, may make more sense for your immediate need than spending time on strategic or system thinking. Alternatively, reading Chapter 7 about decision-making may answer your immediate need. The final three chapters are best read after reading the first eight chapters.

Chapter 1 introduces you to the Integrated Framework for Energizing, Impactful Leadership.

Chapter 2 explains a leader's role in developing and driving purpose, vision, and strategic goals. You will learn how to gain a clear understanding of where your organization needs to be to succeed and, thus, what you want to aspire to achieve.

Chapter 3 explores putting strategic goals in context, which involves system thinking. It explains how to understand the current situation in an organization including organizational history, design, context, characteristics, culture, and readiness for change.

Chapter 4 discusses the importance of self-wisdom including self-awareness, empathy, and mindset. Understanding yourself as a leader requires knowing your strengths and your opportunities for growth, recognizing how you behave under stress, and understanding areas where you have a closed mindset that can hinder effective leadership. Self-reflection is a critical skill for successful leaders.

Chapter 5 explores the impact of your behavior. It discusses the impact of signals you give out as a leader such as authenticity, being present, listening to others, and demonstrating power.

In Chapter 6, you learn how to create a positive environment to maximize your strategy. This chapter discusses how to take advantage of the diverse experiences and ideas of people around you to facilitate creativity and innovation and to create circumstances and conditions that generate positive energy.

Chapters 7 and 8 focus on the fourth element of the Integrated Framework for Energizing, Impactful Leadership: understanding your actions. Chapter 7 covers effective decision-making. Chapter 8 covers conflict and leading change.

Chapters 9 and 10 acknowledge that, in today's connected world, impactful results and actions rarely come from one individual but, rather, involve groups of people. Chapter 9 explores building and managing teams that result in more than the sum of their parts—what I describe as "transcendent teams." Chapter 10 describes a second type of group—alliances, partnerships, or collaborations—involved in delivering results.

Chapter 11 explains how you can create energy to drive change.

It also draws together all the facets of the integrated framework and integrates them into a single approach you can take as a leader. Few people are natural leaders at birth. But almost anyone can become a leader with the right purpose, passion, and the ability to get others to follow their vision.

Becoming an effective leader requires a journey of self-discovery. With this book, you can chart the course of your journey, improve your quality of leadership, increase your and your organization's productivity, and learn how to deliver results with a more engaged, motivated team and collaborators.

Chapter 1
Embracing Energizing, Impactful Leadership

"I am somewhat exhausted: I wonder how a battery feels when it pours electricity into a non-conductor?"

Arthur Conan Doyle
(*The Adventure of the Dying Detective*)

You are reading this book because you want to impact your world; you want to be a great leader. But leadership means different things to different people. Some people view a leader as someone who is a "genius" or "hero," someone who motivates people to take action to change the world around them such as past leaders Winston Churchill, Mahatma Gandhi, or Martin Luther King, Jr. Even some past business leaders are recognized leaders today in improving life for people all around the world, such as Microsoft's co-founder and longtime CEO Bill Gates, who now leads the philanthropic Bill and Melinda Gates Foundation. Others view a leader as someone who is currently at the top of an organization such as Jeff Bezos at Amazon or Elon Musk at Tesla. Or it could be the head of a government.

All the people I just mentioned share the top characteristic of a leader. A leader has a clear, compelling vision of what he or she wants to achieve to help an organization to take advantage of opportunities and overcome challenges—and can motivate others to follow that vision.

Definition of an Energizing, Impactful Leader

What does an energizing, impactful leader look like? These leaders have a strategic vision and deliver on achieving goals for that vision. They build energy that results in a motivated and engaged group of followers who align their actions and behaviors to help deliver the strategic goals.

Delving deeper, energizing, impactful leaders try to impact their world with a specific purpose and strategic goals. They have a vision for achieving the goals. They know they cannot achieve the goals by themselves; they need other people, money, or resources that are outside their control. To deliver their strategic goals, they need people who are willing to follow them, and they need to build energy in their followers. They create energy through the impact of their leadership. Bottom line: Energizing, impactful leadership results in delivering on strategic goals and actions.

Risk of Failure to Deliver

It is dangerous for businesses to disconnect the concept of leadership from the value and results that leaders deliver. Leaders are not successful unless they deliver on goals that result in the business or organization delivering products or services on time, on budget, and with high quality.

You most likely had jobs where leaders were not successful in delivering the desired results. My observation is these situations typically have one of the following outcomes.

Disengaged Failure. In this situation, the leader fails to create energy in the organization and consequently fails to deliver on actions or strategic goals.

Unsustainable Success. Most organizations do not end up with disengaged failure. They deliver their goals in the short term. Often, the leader is very driven. But the energy the leader creates in followers is low and focuses on the short term. The risk with this type of leadership is that people become disengaged, and the top talent may leave.

Dynamic Underachievement. In this type of situation, the leader creates high energy but fails to deliver on goals.

I worked with several organizations that fluctuate between dynamic underachievement and unsustainable success. They are high-energy organizations that fall short of delivering their potential, or their leaders focus on short-term goals that result in burnout.

In contrast to these failure situations, organizations with energized, impactful leaders deliver their strategic goals in a sustained way. The leader drives for short-term results but also creates energy for long-term goals.

Integrated Framework for Energizing, Impactful Leadership

Leadership books and studies typically focus on leadership behaviors, context leadership, transformational leadership, transcendent leadership, ethics and moral development, biology and neuroscience, and systems leadership. These leadership aspects provide some valuable lessons. But they fail to provide all the information you need to become an energizing, impactful leader because they do not integrate all the ideas from all aspects of organizational life.

Becoming an energizing and impactful leader requires developing strength in the four elements displayed in the framework in Figure 1.

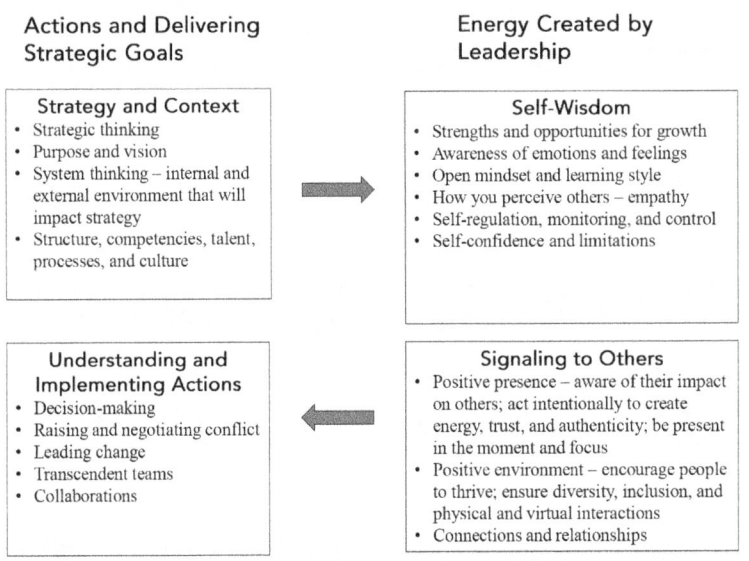

Figure 1 - Integrated Framework for Energizing, Impactful Leaders

As the diagram shows, energizing, impactful leaders are clear about their strategic goals in the context of their purpose and system. They have a high degree of self-wisdom. They signal to others in a way that influences them and builds effective relationships. Finally, they understand actions that deliver and implement their strategies.

It is not possible to be an effective leader if you lack one of the four elements. Lack of any element may derail a leader and lead to not delivering the desired strategic outcome. Effective leaders balance all four elements—strategy, self, relationships, and actions. This can be a complex balance, but this book simplifies the journey of understanding how to balance these elements.

This integrated framework takes a holistic, system approach to leadership. It considers the concepts that make up energizing, impactful leadership. It also considers the short-term and long-term challenges individuals face in taking on a leadership role.

The framework presents a sequence of steps leaders may take including defining a strategy, identifying the context for that strategy, understanding their signals to others, and understanding and implementing actions necessary for delivering on the strategy and leading to the desired results. The integrated framework brings together all facets of leadership and management.

Challenges That Cause Leaders to Fall Behind

Leaders today face new and complex challenges that can cause them to fall behind in achieving their goals. Addressing these challenges requires developing leadership skills in an integrated way. So, you can benefit from the Integrated Framework for Energizing, Impactful Leadership.

Leaders must work interdependently with their colleagues. Today's leadership situations seem like more of a cooperative venture. A major challenge is managing complex, virtual networks of employees and/or contractors that report to the leader as well as external alliance partners and third-party service providers.

This situation of virtual workers became even more complex during the COVID-19 pandemic crisis in 2020, as companies shifted employees to work from home. Although it was an immediate solution during the initial shutdown phase of the crisis, many companies now recognize there are benefits in the work-at-home model. Thus, they consider extending this model for several months or even including it as a permanent model for some of their operations. Leaders must solve new risks for privacy or confidentiality data breaches in virtual situations. Leaders who can overcome the challenges of working virtually are most effective in delivering innovative products and services to market.

In these virtual situations, a leader's influencing skills are more valuable in achieving results than using traditional authoritative power.

Another significant challenge for leaders today is that they often are "in transition." They must prepare for their next role, transition into new roles (internally or externally), or drive complex organizational change due to such situations as reorganization, mergers or divestitures, downsizing, automating, and digital transformation.

Becoming an effective leader requires managing these transitions carefully. The first few months are crucial to sustained success. People rarely have a second chance to make a first impression, and it is difficult to recover from mistakes in the early days.

Communications are another challenge. Leaders often become overwhelmed by what is on their plate for immediate action. Technology now brings levels of connectivity that could only be dreamed of a few years ago. But constant emails and instant messages take up a lot of the day.

Identifying opportunities and creating a follower group is more complex than it used to be. Leaders now have access to ideas, experiences, and skills from people around the world. They now have access to levels of knowledge, data, information sharing, and understanding that lead to true opportunities for insights into solving problems. However, constant communications can become so overwhelming that leaders forget about the need to develop themselves and their teams to deal with the challenges of the future.

Finally, leaders are under pressure to constantly improve their own productivity and their teams' productivity. In addition, they must take action to ensure a high level of productivity from employees working at home. The business environment changes rapidly, and productivity and innovation must increase to meet this dynamic situation.

In your efforts to become a more effective leader, the Integrated Framework for Energizing, Impactful Leaders will help you avoid falling behind because of the leadership challenges described in this chapter. The framework will help you form a road map for addressing the challenges and is a way of tracking your progress on your journey of developing your skills.

Chapter 2

Understanding Your Purpose and Vision: Strategic Thinking

"If wise, a commander is able to recognize changing circumstances and act expediently. If sincere, his men will have no doubt of the certainty of rewards and punishments. If humane, he loves mankind, sympathizes with others, and appreciates their industry and toil. If courageous, he gains victory by seizing opportunity without hesitation."

Sun Tzu
(The Art of War)

Before you begin any journey, it is important to understand where you want to go. I am not against setting out on the road with no clear aim in mind to experience the road and meander through the country lanes on the weekend. But if you want to impact the world or be productive, my experience is that it is critical to have a purposeful strategy and plan and have a clear idea of what success will look like. The first element of the integrated framework described in Chapter 1 focuses on understanding your strategy, where you want to be to be successful, and what you aspire to achieve.

Effective leaders use strategic thinking to know the purpose that drives them and creates energy in themselves and others. Understanding strategy is an analytical process that uses data to identify changing environments and plot the course to achieve the mission and vision. If these elements are not clear, an organization can lack direction and a navigation system.

CHARLES S. DORMER

What is Strategic Thinking?

According to Merriam-Webster Dictionary, strategy is "a careful plan or method for achieving a particular goal usually over a long period of time." From a medical point of view, it is "an adaptation or complex adaptations (as of behaviors, metabolism, or structure) that serves or appears to serve an important function in achieving evolutionary success."

Strategy has its roots in military use. Merriam-Webster Dictionary also defines strategy as "the science and art of employing the political, economic, psychological, and military forces of a nation or group of nations to afford the maximum support to adopted policies in peace and war." Further, strategy is "the science and art of military command exercised to meet the enemy in combat under advantageous conditions."

Dictionary.com draws the distinction between strategy and tactics. "Strategy is the utilization, during both peace and war, of all of a nation's forces, through large-scale, long-range planning and development, to ensure security or victory. Tactics deals with the use and deployment of troops in actual combat."

Two elements in the definition of strategy are important when considering strategic leadership. First, it recognizes a goal (strategic intent). It starts by having a clear understanding of the purpose, mission, and vision for an organization, portfolio, project, or yourself as a leader. Your strategic intent also includes a strategic goal, and a clear understanding of what success will look like if you achieve the goal.

The second element of a strategy is a plan or method (strategic planning). This is a large-scale, long-range plan that starts with a clear understanding of the current situation. You should base your plan on how you will fill the gap between the current and desired state to achieve the strategic intent.

Strategic thinking is the cognitive process that you will apply in the context of defining and implementing a plan to achieve your desired set of long-term goals, as outlined in the definition of strategy described above. It is important that you think about strategy in addition to the tactics to be successful in achieving goals. Strategic thinking involves bringing clarity to a complex situation where the future may be too uncertain to define a way forward.

An important component of strategic thinking is using analytical tools to understand the external environment, including your organization's competition. Strategic thinking should be primarily a data-driven and intelligence-driven process. It uses data to predict how the future state relates to overarching goals. Strategic thinking should be ambitious and involve stretch goals. If you are not ambitious when you develop goals, you run the risk of maintaining the status quo.

Finally, strategic thinking needs to be dynamic and responsive. The external environment changes rapidly today, and a strategic leader needs to be flexible and agile to respond to this dynamic environment.

Levels of Strategy

You can apply a strategy at an organizational, portfolio, product, or individual level. For instance, you may develop a grand strategy that applies to the whole organization. Or you can create a strategy for a part of the organization such as the strategic plan for the approach to a department. You also may develop a strategy that relates to part of the business (such as a strategy in a pharmaceutical company to discover new oncology drugs). Finally, you could create a strategy for a specific project (such as a pharmaceutical company's strategy for developing compound X through clinical trials). Each type of strategy is a long-range, large-scale plan aimed at achieving a goal.

Organizational Level Strategy. This strategy defines a large-scale goal and a strategic plan for an organization. In this context, an "organization" means a group of people who come together in a formal structure such as a company, academic group, or nonprofit organization.

For example, a pharmaceutical company's strategy may include the markets that the company wants to pursue such as pharmaceuticals, medical devices, or over-the-counter products. For a research organization, the strategy may include the types of drugs the company wants to pursue such as large molecules, small molecules, or vaccines. There also may be a company-wide strategy that is specific to an individual marketplace such as a strategy to increase sales in China.

Organizational strategies also can relate to building an organization to deliver a future state. An example is a research group that wants to build competencies and technologies that operate in a virtual way through collaborations and alliances with other companies, academic groups, or other types of organizations. Or an organizational strategy may be to build business growth through mergers and acquisitions of other companies.

Portfolio-Level Strategy. At this level, a company may have a strategy that defines which product lines it will develop, which will be the focus of company efforts.

Product-Level Strategy. At this level, a company may have a strategy for positioning its products in a competitive marketplace. For example, the strategy may be around ensuring a product is less expensive than competitors' products. Or the strategy may be around how to deliver different value to a customer or access a subsegment of a market in a different way.

Individual-Level Strategy. Here, an individual may define a strategy to be more effective as a leader.

To be an effective, energizing, impactful leader, you need the ability to think strategically at all or most of these levels.

A strategy should include a large-scale, long-range, future-focused goal (strategic goal) and a plan (strategic plan) to deliver on that goal. In combination with a clear, well-defined strategy, there also must be operational efficiency for the strategy to be successful. A strategy is just a pipe dream if it lacks actions that deliver the strategic promise.

The Importance of Purpose

A critical piece of formulating a strategy is knowing where you want to go. In other words, what is the overarching goal? There are several ways to answer this question. The answer may be as simple as "being first to market" or "increasing sales of our product." It becomes more complicated when you develop a grand strategy for your organization or for yourself as a leader. The complication arises because you need to communicate the purpose.

Aspiring journalists learn early that they need to explain the "5 Ws"—the who, what, where, when, and why of a happening they write about so readers will know what is important. As a leader, you need to drive change in an organization. But you will not succeed at inspiring followers to take action unless you inspire them with the purpose for change. The purpose also creates a clear focus for determining what actions to take.

Knowing Your Purpose Ensures Clear Focus

Let me illustrate the value of your purpose by sharing my experience in the pharmaceutical industry. Before I joined my first pharmaceutical company, I worked with hospitals and knew my purpose was to help patients. I fixed clearly in my mind the image of a sick child who cried with pain in the middle of the night, perhaps due to an ear infection or something more serious. I knew that the best hope for relieving the child's suffering was medicine and, more specifically, drugs to relieve the pain and potentially cure the underlying disease.

It was an important mission for me to work in an environment that researched innovative treatments for patients, and I joined a drug company with that mission in mind. That was my purpose. The reason I got up in the morning was to work for an organization to get new drugs to patients.

An experience with a colleague strengthened my commitment to this mission. My colleague (I will call her Zhang in this book) was a young woman who was diagnosed with breast cancer a few years before I met her. She was the bravest person I ever met. For the five years I knew her, she battled the awful disease and tried every experimental drug available.

The battle with the disease and the side effects of the drugs left her sick, exhausted, and weak. But she showed up for work every single day. I had many conversations with her, suggesting she take some time off and rest. But she always said "no." Late one Friday afternoon, as I packed up my computer to go home, Zhang appeared at my door. I remember it as though it were yesterday. She said, "I think I will take some time off next week, and I won't be in on Monday." Of course, I said that I was pleased to hear that she was doing that and that I would see her soon. But as she walked away, I knew that I would not see her again. She passed away a few weeks later.

I called our head of research for oncology and told him that we had to fix this problem and we could not have women suffering and dying from this devastating disease. Of course, that was already obvious to a person who spent his life fighting cancer in his research. My sense of powerlessness heightened my sense of urgency and focus for my purpose in my job.

As a leader, it is important that you know the overarching purpose, the reason why you do something. That mission gives you energy and focus. Whether you work in a large organization or a small one, it is easy to become distracted from your mission. The constant flow of email, meetings, gossip about the next merger, or any number of other distractions can fill your day and use up your energy.

In the case of drug research and development, it is also easy to be distracted from the mission because the development time for drugs spreads over many years. It is sometimes easy to forget the overarching mission when getting a drug to patients may not happen for several years.

A clear focus and mission create energy in you and motivate you to get up in the morning. This is particularly true if the purpose is based on an emotion and has a direct connection with you.

Clearly, my experience with Zhang was highly emotional for me, which is why it is so clear and deeply remembered. One impact of my clear focus occurred in meetings I attended. If I could not see the link between the meeting and getting drugs to patients in the first fifteen minutes, I quietly left and did something else with my time. A second impact was that I made sure the decision-makers were in the room for a meeting. If they were not there, I saw little point to the meeting. As an effective leader, you need to focus your time on achieving your purpose.

However, some tasks or jobs may not have a direct impact on the mission. For example, I had roles in my career that involved business redesign; these roles were not directly involved in getting drugs to patients. In those times, I best served my mission by making the organization as effective as possible and ensuring that inefficiency did not cause us to miss opportunities to fund new drugs.

By having a clear purpose statement, you can maintain a focus of how you can avoid becoming distracted. I will further discuss not being distracted from your focus and "being present" in another chapter.

Knowing Your Purpose Inspires Others to Follow

Several common terms when talking about the purpose of an organization include strategic intent, mission, vision, and reason for being. These points are important because they inspire others to follow the organization's purpose. To succeed as an energizing, impactful leader, you need to not only manage people to achieve goals but also inspire them to be engaged and motivated.

For example, during my time in the pharmaceutical industry, I saw many change initiatives to address the productivity problem: R&D cycle time reduction, "shots on goal" portfolio management, mergers and acquisitions, and building new discovery technologies and competencies, to mention just a few. These potential solutions may have been effective; so, companies spent a lot of time and effort in implementing them.

The leadership challenge was to inspire people to change the way they worked and increase their effectiveness and efficiency. The purpose for these organizations was clear: creating a healthier world. It was a clear purpose that inspired people to get involved with this mission. Increasing productivity was not just about making more money; it was about the health of the world. Leaders communicated this vision repeatedly and consistently over many years to produce alignment across the organization and inspire people to do their best even through times of great change.

Developing Strategic Goals

Your purpose relates to the passion that motivates you to get up in the morning, whether it is your individual purpose, your vision for a portfolio or project, or your organization's mission. Often, it can have a strong emotional element. Setting a strategic goal is more rational, and you should base it on rational thinking and acting on knowledge and intelligence. Base it on an analysis of the external environment and predicting what your place can be in the future.

One of the most famous strategic goals set by a leader was President John F. Kennedy's space goal announced in 1962. At that time, the United States was behind in a space race with the then USSR. The USSR launched the first man into space in April 1961. This event tested the US assumption that it was the world leader in technology and science. John F. Kennedy then made a now-famous speech in 1962, which included the following quote:

> "We choose to go to the moon. We choose to go to the moon in this decade and do the other things, not because they are easy, but because they are hard, because that goal will serve to organize and measure the best of our energies and skills, because that challenge is one that we are willing to accept, one we are unwilling to postpone, and one which we intend to win, and the others, too."

This speech is clearly a strategic goal and defines a clear outcome: landing a man on the moon and returning him safely to Earth. It also had a clear timeline: within the next decade. It was an ambitious and stretch goal. I can imagine that engineers and scientists at NASA at the time knew the huge challenge this goal represented. It aligned with the mission of the United States: to be the leader of the world. Finally, it created a sense of urgency: unwilling to postpone the goal.

From my experience, when formulating a strategic goal, you should have a clear vision of what success will look like if you achieve the goal. For example, in the case of Kennedy's goal for the United States, success would be measured by having a man walk on the moon and return safely to Earth. People could visualize this outcome, and the impact of such an image would clearly demonstrate what he described as the "best energies and skills" in the United States.

A strategic goal for your organization, product, portfolio, or for yourself should include what you aim to achieve in the context of your marketplace and competitors.

In the case of Kennedy's strategic goal, the primary customers were the people of the United States who, through their taxes, would pay for the moonshot. Representing the people were politicians in Congress who would need to approve the budget for NASA. If Kennedy lacked public and political support, his idea of a moonshot would, quite literally, not get off the ground. The competition in the situation was not only the USSR but also other groups in the United States that competed for the same research funds. Kennedy's strategic goal relied on getting funds at the expense of other projects.

As you develop a strategic goal, you need to identify your customers, your market, and your competitors. This requires understanding the external environment in which your organization operates. A key leadership skill is analyzing the external environment so that you can identify trends and patterns in the marketplace and understand your organization's customers and their problems.

Initial Steps in Strategic Planning

To succeed as an effective leader, you first need to understand what your strategy should be. In other words, you need to develop the strategic intent for the organization. You need to know your "target," that is, where you want to be in the long term. This incorporates the mission, purpose, strategic intent, and strategic goals for the organization.

The next action is to specify plans to achieve the strategic goal. The aim of your strategic plan is to animate and bring to life the strategic intent and strategic goals. You need to take the following steps when developing strategic goals. First, perform a "gap" analysis between where you are currently and where you want to be. Next, formulate mid-range goals that move toward longer-term goals. The third step is to identify risks and plans to mitigate those risks in implementing mid-range goals. Finally, you need to identify measures that will show whether the plans are working.

Understanding your current situation involves having an in-depth knowledge of your organization's competencies, structure, assets (intellectual property), people, and leadership capabilities. I will explain this step more extensively in Chapter 3, which looks at using a system-based approach to understand an organization's current situation.

By analyzing the current situation and the desired future state (strategic goal), your gap analysis shows areas for growth and development. Chapter 3 also provides details about other steps such as setting mid-range goals, assessing risk, creating risk-mitigation plans, and developing appropriate metrics to assess whether the plan works.

Energizing, Impactful Leadership in Action: Purpose and Vision

It was late on a Friday afternoon, but Sari was not ready to pack up her things and head home. She was full of energy and ideas. In fact, in her two years at the company, she could not remember a time when she felt more alive and engaged. She was Head of Research and Development for a mid-sized drug company that built its reputation on discovering, developing, and marketing drugs for rare diseases.

The reason for her energy that Friday was because of attending a three-day Advisory Group meeting with leading experts in different fields of research and treatment of rare diseases. Sari and her team presented their research strategies for multiple diseases they pursued. She set the meeting to get input and advice as to their strategies and to get an understanding of the most cutting-edge thinking and ideas outside her company. During the meeting, they also heard from patients who emphasized how desperate they were for treatments for their diseases.

From the discussions over the three days, Sari realized there were enormous opportunities to impact patients' lives, which filled her with energy and enthusiasm. She also recognized the huge challenges ahead for her team.

Sari reflected on why this meeting was such a success for her and her team. When she became Head of Research and Development, she focused most of her time on getting to know the strengths and weaknesses of the organization she inherited and the science of the assets in the pipeline. It was a steep learning curve for her, and she had to make some urgent organizational changes related to delivering on the key milestones. Mired in the details of daily operations, she had little time to think strategically about where the organization needed to be.

Thinking strategically, she realized the purpose and vision for her team was to work on the diseases for a better life for the patients who relied on her team to help solve their medical needs. She knew that this needed to be her focus and she had to minimize distractions that would stand in the way of achieving this purpose. She also needed to inspire her organization to follow her in achieving this mission.

Following the Advisory Group meeting, she began thinking strategically and thinking about the future of their research. She also started thinking about the external environment, specifically industry trends, opportunities, and threats.

The next week, Sari called a meeting of her leadership team to discuss the company strategy. Their challenge was defining strategic goals. They brainstormed ideas to identify a strategic goal that would apply to their organization, products, and portfolio of research assets. They wanted to identify a goal that would align with the organization's mission and purpose.

After a lot of discussion, the leadership team arrived at their strategic goal. Sari knew that if they achieved this strategic goal, they would achieve her purpose and strategic intent and they could have a real impact on patients' lives.

Sari and her leadership team also spent time considering what success would look like in five years. From the organization's perspective, they would have the best talent in the fields of science that they investigated. They also would succeed in forming and managing collaborations and partnerships to deliver results. As part of that objective, they would be the partner of choice. Success from the product and portfolio perspective meant they would deliver innovative products and be first to the market using novel approaches in disease areas not served by therapies and drugs.

Sari knew they were off to a great start. The strategic goal would evolve over time, but this was a good first draft. The next step for her and the team would be developing strategic plans to achieve their strategic goal. They would need to start the process of gaining knowledge and intelligence and deep dive into customer needs and the market for rare diseases. She knew they needed a clear understanding of the current science and their competitors.

She also recognized she would need a clear understanding of her organization's strengths and weaknesses. And she began thinking about her personal strategic goal as a strategic leader.

Sari felt energized by the challenge of her mission. If she failed to inspire her team, she would generate negative energy that would come from an unclear vision and strategy, lack of clarity on where the organization was going, and confusion about how her team fit in the organization. However, she was confident that she could create positive energy by having a clear purpose, clarity on what they wanted to achieve, and how they could have an impact on the world.

Thinking strategically as she left work that Friday night, she realized that her first task must be generating energy in her team around a clear purpose. She identified why her organization existed and what they aimed to achieve. The next step would be defining specific strategies to achieve this intent and goal.

Chapter Summary

To succeed as an energizing, impactful leader, you need to use strategic thinking and understand your strategy. The strategy for an organization, product, portfolio, or you as a leader represents a clear understanding of where you want to go.

Thinking strategically is a key leadership skill. This thinking starts by developing a strategic intent around why the organization exists, its purpose and mission, and the vision. Often, the purpose is based on an emotional connection to a problem that needs a solution.

Your purpose is important, as it leads to a clear focus in how to create and use energy. It is also important because you will use it to inspire others to follow and be part of your dream. In other words, it creates energy and focus for others.

A strategic intent will be just a dream unless it links to clear strategic goals (such as Kennedy's intent of "shooting for the moon"). Identifying strategic goals is not based solely on emotions; it also requires analysis of strengths and weaknesses of the internal world (whether it is an organization, a product, a portfolio, or having a strong awareness of yourself). It also requires analyzing the external environment for such factors as current trends and challenges, identifying the competition and what they do, and identifying the marketplace.

You may base strategic goals on a unique set of skills or attributes that you have, which lead to a unique value proposition or unique way of solving customers' problems.

Key Learnings About Strategic Thinking

- Energizing, impactful leaders are strategic thinkers, as they know their purpose that drives them and creates energy.
- They have clear and powerful strategic goals that focus their energy and inspire others to follow.
- Their purpose evokes an emotional response in themselves and others.

- They are analytical in identifying their goals; they understand the opportunities and challenges in their internal and external environments that will impact their strategy.

Action Plan for Improving Strategic Thinking

In your action plan, take time to reflect on your strengths and your opportunity for growth. This self-reflection has two parts. First, review the following questions and rate yourself for a strength or an opportunity for growth for each question. Next, think about actions that you can take to enhance your strength or develop your opportunity for growth.

1. Can you identify your purpose for your organization, product, or yourself?
2. Do you focus the majority of your time on your purpose?
3. Do you inspire others to follow your vision and purpose?
4. Do you think about the external environment and competition and identify opportunities and challenges that will impact your strategy?
5. Do you challenge the status quo in your organization and push back on the way people perform processes and tasks?
6. Do you look for new insights and innovative approaches to solving customers' problems?
7. Do you have clarity about your strategic goals and those of your organization?

Chapter 3
Developing Strategic Goals in Context: System Thinking

"A problem never exists in isolation; it is surrounded by other problems in space and time. The more of the context of a problem that a scientist can comprehend, the greater are his chances of finding a truly adequate solution."

Russell L. Ackoff
(organizational theorist, consultant, author)

Energizing, impactful leaders use strategic thinking to determine their purpose and identify where they want to go. This requires using system-thinking skills for both internal and external systems. System thinking will help you understand your organization's current situation including its history, design, context, characteristics, culture, and readiness for change.

Any change to an organization starts from the current context, whether it is organizational structure, organizational characteristics, current portfolio of products and assets, or other factors. If you fail to consider the current situation, you face a significant risk: your change effort can become a theoretical exercise because it is not based on the organization's "real world" situation.

Understanding the current context also gives you an indication of the extent of the change effort that is required to meet the new business strategy. Only by knowing where the organization is today and where it needs to be can you define a strategy to bridge that gap.

Systems are entities with interconnected components or functionalities. Companies design the components to create optimal outcomes. Think, for instance, about the Amazon online platform and business. Its platform is a system enabling customers to shop and purchase the items they want, and even discover suggested related items they may not have thought of. Components enable such functionalities as integrating stored data about a customer's typical purchases and buying patterns, pushing product descriptions to potential buyers, seamlessly and quickly executing the financial transaction, and managing a customer's privacy. If the platform lacked any of those components, the system would not deliver optimal results and customer satisfaction.

Similarly, your organization may have the best strategies for individual departments, but the whole system will not produce a highly productive organization unless leaders design those departmental strategies with the organization's overall functionality in mind. The design challenge is not about how good the individual parts are but how they fit together and work as a system to deliver the optimal result. Leaders must optimize how the individual parts work together.

When considering your organization, system thinking considers the whole organization, the interdependencies and interconnections within the organization, and its external environment. How does the organization interact and interconnect with its internal entities and its external environment? I refer to this system thinking as optimizing the effectiveness of organizational interconnections and interfaces.

As an energizing, impactful leader, you also need to understand the context of your organization's current situation while you define strategic goals. In other words, you need to understand your starting point, the resources, and competencies you have, and what you need to develop or acquire to be successful. As I mentioned earlier, if you embark on a strategy without considering your current system based on the organization's real-world situation, there is a danger your journey will become just a theoretical exercise.

System thinking brings the context to a strategy. It gives

understanding to the current and possible future states of an organization and its external environment.

Keep in mind, in a fast-changing environment, the system is not static; it changes dynamically. To ensure your effectiveness as a leader, you need to constantly monitor the system and make adjustments to strategy in real time.

System thinking is primarily an analytical way of thinking and involves obtaining data about the internal system and the external environment. It involves looking for patterns and trends in these data to define the best strategy to deliver on an organization's strategic intent and goals. A popular way of framing this kind of analysis is a SWOT analysis, which defines strengths, weaknesses, opportunities, and threats. A later section of this book, which discusses strategic planning, includes information on using a SWOT analysis.

Understanding Your Organization

As discussed above, it is important to have a clear, in-depth understanding of your organization's status. This is the starting point for a new strategy and should form a framework for an ongoing assessment. This, in combination with a clear strategic goal and vision of what success would look like, allows an analysis of the gaps that you need to fill to deliver the new strategy. From this gap analysis, you can define specific strategic plans.

To conduct your organization's assessment, I suggest using a framework consisting of three elements: organizational design, organizational characteristics, and organizational conditions.

Organizational Design

Organizational design describes what the organization currently looks like such as the structure, the people, and resources available, and the organization's competencies. The analysis of the organization design should be a full inventory of what comprises the organization. There are several ways to look at the design, but I suggest the framework shown in Figure 2.

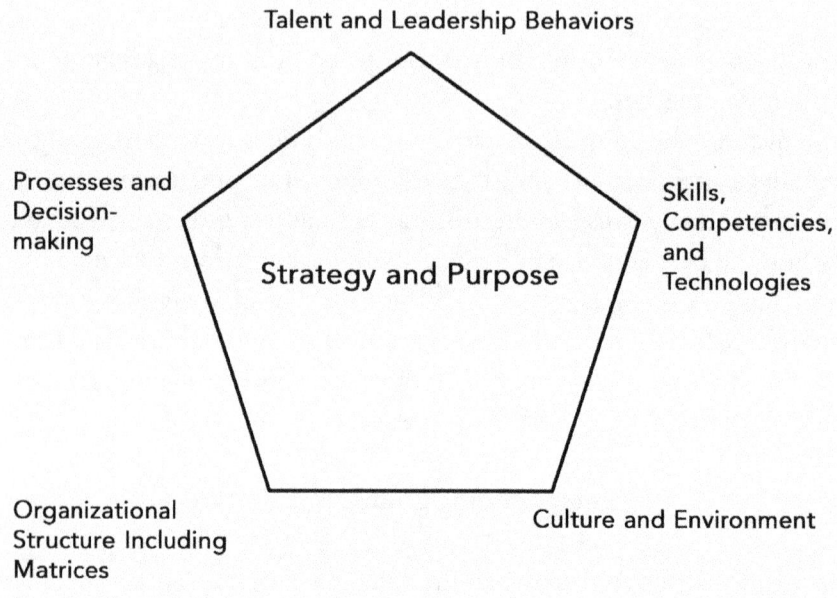

Figure 2 – Five Dimensions of an Organization

The best way to assess these five parts of an organization is by considering the following questions regarding each of the five dimensions shown in Figure 2.

Dimension 1. How are the members of the organization segmented into departments, divisions, etc.? How is the team (matrix) structure organized?

These organizational structures usually appear in the form of organization charts with interconnected boxes and reporting relationships. This inventory of the organization structure and team matrix also will show the resources available. The assessment should include a clear understanding of budgets, facilities, equipment, and all the elements represented by the "hardwiring" of the organization.

The assessment also should include an inventory of all external relationships (collaborations, supplier partnerships, licensing deals, joint ventures, and other alliances). For a large, complex organization, this assessment can be a significant undertaking and generate a lot of data, but it is important to occasionally take stock of the organization's inventory.

Dimension 2. What are the key processes that drive the business? These processes represent how the activities of the individuals and teams are connected and optimized. In most organizations, a key process that should be defined is how decisions are made and who has decision rights and accountability for each decision.

Dimension 3. What is the organization's culture and environment? These are behavioral norms for the organization and the work environment. (This will be discussed in more detail later in this chapter.)

Dimension 4. What skills, competencies, and technologies does the organization have to execute its strategy? For example, in a pharmaceutical company, this may include specific expertise in the research field or patented technology for drug delivery.

Dimension 5. Who are the key talent and effective strategic leaders? The assessment should include an inventory of the members of the organization who are critical to delivering the strategy. These are staff members the organization cannot afford to lose. It is also valuable to have development plans for those people as well as well-developed succession plans.

Once you have an in-depth understanding of your current organizational design (current state), the next step is to identify the organizational design that is required to deliver your strategic intent and strategic goals (future state). In a similar way to assessing the current state, the future-state analysis should answer the following questions related to the five dimensions.

First, what is the optimal way of organizing the members of the organization into departments, divisions, etc.? How should the team (matrix) structure be organized? Second, what processes need to be standardized and agreed upon? What decision-making processes are required?

Next, what culture or environment needs to be established to deliver the strategic goals? Further, what skills, competencies, and technology does the organization need to execute the strategy? And, finally, what talent and leadership behaviors need to be part of the organization?

These dimensions represent the system of elements in an organization that come together and, if applied in a system way, complement each other and lead to transformational change.

If you do not view these dimensions as a whole and change them independently of each other, the risk is that the system will not be balanced, and the impact will deliver only incremental improvements. When making design decisions, you must design the organization using a system approach that integrates all dimensions and that has the maximum impact on the whole system. For example, process design without changes in leadership behaviors or the culture will not change the whole system for the better and may make it worse.

Organizational Characteristics

Several organizational characteristics should be part of an analysis of the current state. The first point to consider is the maturity of the organization. This is important to understand because the maturity stage presents different challenges and opportunities for strategic leaders.

Consider a start-up company, for instance. Its leaders face challenges in creating an initial business plan, obtaining venture capital funding, and building a viable organization. Start-ups tend to not have a great interest in leadership productivity as they focus heavily on product development and getting to market. However, there is an opportunity for development of leaders in a start-up because bad leadership can have a major impact on the organization and implementing the business plan. The impact of a leader's behavior, either good or bad, is bigger in a small company.

Leaders in more mature companies have opportunities for coaching interventions and face transition-phase challenges. These companies achieve an initial degree of success as a start-up and are in the process of expanding. The organization's leaders need to manage the transition as the company grows in size and complexity. Often, the founder or co-founders of a start-up lack the necessary leadership skills to transition the company for further growth. This presents an opportunity for coaching.

As companies mature, the organization often becomes relatively large and bureaucratic. Growth slows, and the company may tend to live off its past success. Leaders in these organizations face challenges because of a highly complex and political culture. There is an opportunity for leaders to grow to have an impact.

Organizations can grow to a point where they may see decline and may need to transition to another business. At this stage, leaders face challenges because of the organization's defensive mode. Unless the company manages to transition to a new business, it may atrophy into nonexistence. Leaders in these organizations often focus on the challenge of downsizing as resources become tighter and tighter. Activities such as training and coaching shift lower on the priority list. This is, of course, counter-intuitive to what the leader needs to do to spur new growth.

As an energizing, impactful leader, you should have a good understanding of your organization's maturity and life-cycle stage. There are several sweet spots for leadership and strategy definition, particularly in growth companies where changes in leadership behavior can help leaders and companies take advantage of this growth. However, there is also an opportunity for leaders to have an impact in all other phases of the business cycle.

When assessing the current state, another important organizational characteristic is the portfolio of products and assets the organization owns. In the broadest sense and independent of the type of organization, people, and other resources (finances, facilities, etc.) comprise and define an organization. Intellectual property (IP) also defines the organization. Intellectual property includes patents, copyrights, publications, and all assets in the company that are protected and of particular importance in the case of science and technology.

From a strategic-planning perspective, a leader must undertake an assessment of current intellectual property. As with the other organizational characteristics, the assessment should include a clear understanding of what intellectual property needs to be developed to reach the organization's strategic goals. Strategic plans should include how the gap between the current IP position and the future desired position will be developed and in what time frame.

It is important to apply an external view of the company's portfolio of products and research assets. Leaders should frame the strategic plan in the context of the external marketplace. "Marketplace" in this context may be a commercial market for drugs, medical devices, technologies, or a marketplace for ideas in a field of science and technology.

An in-depth analysis of the competition in the market in terms of current market and future markets is a key driver for strategic planning. Each asset in the portfolio should have a clear target population for a product or technology as well as a complete analysis of competitors' products or technologies that are currently in the market or in research and development. The same principle applies to other commercial ventures in science and technology and non-commercial organizations. Having a broad and deep assessment of the work in a field will help to position an organization's research assets.

Assessing the products and research assets should be an ongoing process, and reassessment of product or research assets should occur as new data emerge from the external environment. Taking a system approach to assessing both internal and external opportunities and challenges is key to strategic planning.

Organizational Conditions

Another aspect of analyzing an organization's current state is assessing its organizational conditions. This relates to the current environment in the organization and the levels of engagement of the people in it. Employee engagement is a key driver of productivity and often determines whether a company can retain key talent. There are multiple approaches to understanding employee engagement, and one of the most popular and valuable tools is to survey employees on critical questions.

This is, of course, a much easier task with SurveyMonkey and other survey tools now available online.

The mood of an organization can change quickly as the organization changes both positively and negatively. Leaders should be aware of the "temperature" of their organization. The organization's mood can significantly affect the impact of strategic leaders.

An interesting aspect of organizational mood is that change produces a high level of uncertainty in people going through change. Clearly, restructuring resulting in job loss greatly magnifies uncertainty. If this is happening, it may cause people to be concerned about how they will feed their family if they are laid off. They may also have concerns around safety in terms of their job security and stability.

Having been involved in several downsizing experiences, my observation is that it also significantly impacts social aspects. Key parts of an employee's social network may be removed because of downsizing, and it disrupts established social networks within the organization.

Even people who remain in the organization will have concerns and be disrupted. This is illustrated by the concept of "survivor guilt." They feel guilty about surviving when their colleagues and, in some cases, friends lose their jobs. It will affect their self-esteem, and self-actualization may be difficult.

Therefore, when you consider your organization's conditions, it is important to understand the change environment and the levels of uncertainty around job security. Understanding changes that recently happened and are about to happen is important from a strategic-planning perspective.

As an example, an organization can carry the scars of past changes, and people may become risk averse and gun shy if they experience a lot of change. They may be paralyzed with the thought that they are waiting for the "next shoe to drop." I worked with people who experienced multiple reorganizations. One person with whom I worked had three different supervisors in two years. The impact of such constant change can make it difficult to plan for the future. One person joked that the current reorganization does not matter because reorganization will happen again in six months.

Organizational Leadership Style

One of the biggest influencing factors that determines whether a leader can succeed is understanding the leadership style that is prevalent in an organization.

Some important features of leadership that create positive energy include listening and providing feedback, creating a safe environment, taking a long-term view, defining common ground, raising the bar, showing appreciation, creating pride, establishing clear roles and responsibilities, assuming others do their best, knowing that vulnerability is not weakness, being a system advocate, and demonstrating a code of honor. Looking for these characteristics in leaders in an organization will help you determine if the coaching environment is friendly or not.

The opposite situation is also true. Leaders who create a blame culture, discourage risk-taking, focus on the short term, are not appreciative, do not give honest feedback, settle for average performance, give unclear roles and responsibilities, victimize weakness, have silo thinking, and cannot be trusted create negative energy.

As part of assessing your organization's current condition, you can conduct employee surveys about the impact of leadership styles and behavior. Survey questions should focus on the impact of leaders' behavior. For instance, do leaders encourage innovation through their behaviors? Do leaders foster employee development and engagement? Do leaders inspire optimism, spirit, and promise? Surveys with questions such as these provide rich data on the condition of the organization, and leaders should conduct them on a regular basis as a health check.

In combination with the current-state assessment, you also need to understand the style of leadership that will create positive energy to deliver the strategic goals. In a similar way to other aspects discussed (organizational character and organizational design), you can conduct a gap analysis and define strategic plans to fill those gaps.

In a later chapter, I will discuss in greater detail more models that illustrate the leadership style of an organization.

Organizational Ability to Change

The final organizational condition you should assess is whether your organization is ready to change. Change management is an important skill for strategic leaders. Delivering strategic goals inevitably will result in the need for an organization to change from its current state to a desired state. I will discuss change management in greater detail in a later chapter.

Changing System Elements

You need to use system thinking in decision-making as it relates to integrated organizational change. Decisions are required on what change is needed, and the intent may be to evolve the current state or radically transform the business. You can change any system's components to reach a desired new state and impact productivity by using the following approaches.

You can, for instance, optimize delivery through changes in organizational structure. You can move the organizational culture and environment to facilitate innovation. Or you may opt to develop leadership behaviors to achieve outcome. Or you can develop ways of working across departments as a matrix (project teams and project management).

Another approach for changing system elements is to implement clear decision rights and governance to move the portfolio of projects. Similarly, you can maximize resource utilization through alignment and prioritization. You may want to access ideas by collaborating both internally and through external alliances and partnerships.

You can decide to manage the business of science effectively by controlling budgets, operations, and legal/compliance. You can also try to maximize the effectiveness of processes and cutting out white space in the way talent delivers projects. Another significant approach is to take steps to attract and retain the best talent who will help achieve goals.

Often, these approaches do not fully achieve the desired outcome. In other cases, the opposite effect may occur. In my experience, leaders tend to pull one or two of the levers independently without a full understanding of the impact on the whole system. For example, to transform an organization at the speed needed to solve the problems with pharmaceutical R&D requires a shift of the whole organization to a new paradigm.

To be an effective leader, you need to use an integrated approach to change. In other words, keep the whole system in mind when changing the parts and change the whole system rather than parts.

A System-Thinking Approach to Strategic Planning

The aims of strategic plans are to animate and bring to life the strategic intent and strategic goal. An effective way to understand what a strategic plan should be is to perform a "gap analysis." Understanding your organization's current situation involves having an in-depth knowledge of your organizational design, characteristics, and conditions. By analyzing the current situation and the desired future state (strategic goal), it is possible to identify areas for growth and development.

Using a system-thinking approach is highly beneficial in deciding which strategies to follow. This applies equally to the strategy that a company wants to follow or a product strategy. There are two pieces of strategy to consider here. First, what is the desired future that you aim to achieve? Second, what is the plan to deliver on this strategy? A system-thinking approach applies to both pieces.

As an example, whether a company defines the strategy for R&D by a linear analysis of the current market, by its projections of future markets (commercial pull), or by the current knowledge of today's science (discovery push), the company can make the mistake of assuming that by studying one part it will be able to predict how the whole system will behave. In other words, a company must formulate its strategy (where it wants to be) by considering that all aspects are part of an open system and avoid the dangers of analyzing a closed system in R&D.

Another popular approach to developing strategic plans is the SWOT analysis. This analysis involves looking at Strengths, Weaknesses, Opportunities, and Threats to an organization. If performed successfully, this is a data-driven, analytical approach that you can apply to your organization's strategy, products, or you as a leader.

The advantage of a SWOT analysis is that you can use it to assess both internal and external environments. You can use this tool to assess a current situation (identifying your organization's current strengths and weaknesses and its current opportunities and threats). You can also use it to define plans for a future state (identifying strengths the organization needs to enhance, how it can overcome weaknesses, and how it can take advantage of opportunities and minimize threats).

Whether you use a gap analysis or a SWOT analysis, it is valuable to define several potential future scenarios. Strategic plans should define these "what if" scenarios based upon several different outcomes. For each gap identified between your current state and the future state needed to deliver your strategic goals, you need a strategic plan.

You could design a strategic plan to deliver the future state in different time frames (such as a three-year or five-year plan). In some cases, it may be ten years or more. The plan should be detailed in terms of what you and your team need to do and in what time frame. Although not as detailed as a tactical plan, the shorter range of the plan should be more detailed.

Your strategic plan also should include mid-range goals that would be stepping-stones in the longer-term plan. The important point here is that your strategic plan should not be static and set in stone. The internal and external environments may be very dynamic; therefore, you should regularly review and update long-term plans to take account of changes in these environments.

Another key part of strategic planning is to have an appreciation of assumptions when putting together the plan and the risks that may be barriers to success. Risk management should be a part of any planning process. Include a strategy to mitigate risk associated with the goals.

Finally, you should build measures to include in the strategic plan to show progress towards the goals. There are a lot of materials available that detail how to put together strategic plans, including some valuable tools. I advise reading these materials.

In addition to using a system-thinking approach when defining strategic plans, you need to use analytical thinking and scientific management. In the case of defining organizational and product strategic plans, be aware that they are part of open systems and you need to define strategy in the context of those systems. This will give benefits in a rapidly changing environment so you can shape the system changes rather than just react to them.

Energizing, Impactful Leadership in Action: Putting Strategic Goals in Context

In the summer of 2012, Mary took a family vacation to Cape Cod and decided to take the short boat ride across to the island of Nantucket, a small slither of sand about thirty miles off the coast of Cape Cod. She visited the Whaling Museum and soon learned the incredible story behind this thriving island community.

That story started her thinking about how Nantucket's history illustrates what happens in a fast-changing business environment. She heard about the history of whaling and the wealth that was created but also how the whaling industry quickly changed and the economic decline that followed.

Through that story, she recognized that, if an organization did not change fast enough, it would not survive in a changing business environment. She concluded that a possible explanation for the Nantucket whaling failure was that the whalers did not react to changes in the system of which they were a part.

Mary was conscious that an organization today needs a strategy to make the most of a changing environment. Thinking about the Nantucket whalers, she appreciated the dangers of looking inwardly into her organization and not appreciating how she as a leader needed to shape strategy by the external environment.

Mary was clear about her role as vice president for oncology research. She lost her mother to cancer. Since then, her passion was to help cancer patients avoid her mother's fate. This was her personal purpose.

Mary worked with her team to develop strategic goals for the oncology research group aimed at "delivering innovative drugs for oncology patients to alleviate pain and suffering and extend the life of these patients." Her team scanned the external environment in the oncology field and recognized trends and opportunities. This analysis gave her a good understanding for her strategy. She knew she needed to focus on the science and technology that revolutionized oncology research but also on operational improvements in the product-development process.

To meet her strategic goals, she knew that her organization would need to change quickly to overcome the R&D productivity dilemma. She needed to transform her organization fundamentally, not just make small incremental improvements.

The next key step for Mary and her team was to work on the strategic plans based on the context of her organization. The important lesson for Mary from her experience in Nantucket was that she needed to develop a system-thinking approach to understand her strategy and strategic plans.

Using that approach, she started from the current context (organizational structure, organizational characteristics, current portfolio of products and assets, and other factors). She understood the current situation based on the history and evolution of her organization and identifying the gap in her strategy. This gave her an indication of the extent of the change effort required to meet the new business strategy. Mary was clear that she needed to develop her skills in system thinking.

Mary started to think about the systems she needed to consider in further defining her strategic goals and strategic plans. She worked for a pharmaceutical company, so she was part of the pharmaceutical industry system. She was involved in oncology research and therefore part of the health care system that treated oncology patients. She was an oncology scientist, so she was part of the scientific and technology field of oncology research. She researched drugs and was therefore part of the oncology market system along with other competitors selling drugs for cancer patients. Working for a large pharmaceutical company, she was also part of the company system. As vice president for oncology research, she was also part of the broader R&D system for the company. Finally, her research department was another system she needed to consider.

Mary realized that no matter how good the analysis of a business and piecemeal changes to part of a system were, they could not overcome the larger challenges the industry faced. She wanted to create an environment and culture where both analytical and system thinking would be encouraged, rewarded, and considered in the formulation of strategy and decision-making.

Mary arranged a series of meetings with her leadership team to discuss the major gaps in organizational design between the current organization and the one they needed to deliver their strategic goal. She even brought in a management consultant firm to help with this process. These meetings were not easy sometimes, as her team was passionate about what they needed.

They did not always agree with each other, but the team reached consensus on the major gaps. Mary and her team identified some gaps in skills. The current organization was strong with skills related to small molecule research and biologists who had a good disease understanding. To be a leader in the field of oncology, they also needed to build a competency in antibody technologies. This was a clear gap, and they needed to build strategic plans to fill that gap and recruit experts in this field.

Another gap the team identified was in the way they made decisions. It was a top-down process with Mary and her leadership team making major decisions. They recognized it as a bureaucratic process, and they received feedback that scientists spent a lot of time and effort in preparing PowerPoint slides for top leaders to make decisions. They needed to be more flexible and faster in making key decisions and empower their project teams to make decisions about how the project should go forward.

This was a real "aha" moment for Mary. She realized that they created a problem for their scientists and wasted valuable time. She wanted her scientists to focus on the science and getting drugs to cancer patients, not on becoming PowerPoint experts. A key point in their strategic plans would be defining decision-making processes that would be rigorous but simple.

The leadership team identified another gap: they needed a culture that encouraged and rewarded innovation and was open to new ideas and "thinking outside the box." An assessment of the current organization showed that the culture was hierarchical and traditional in the way people thought. Past leadership did not encourage people to take risks and penalized people if they failed.

Mary knew that if they were going to be innovative in their approaches there would be risk and some projects would fail. The important thing is that they learn from these failures and build those lessons learned into new projects. This was a big gap in their culture and needed to change and become part of the strategic plans they formulated.

Finally, Mary was aware that she needed to build her leadership team and develop the talent that would enable her organization to meet the new challenges. Gaps in the organization would require some new talent joining the company. In addition, each of her leaders needed a development plan to build their strategic leadership skills.

After one of these meetings, Mary reflected on the progress she made with her team. She felt good about the fact that they had a much better picture of her current department and had a vision of the organization design elements they would need to meet her strategic goals.

The major gaps they identified were all important to fill, but she saw the real power across the gaps as a system. She needed to develop her leadership talent to lead a more innovative culture with fast, flexible, simple decision-making to build competencies in new technologies. Mary had the first piece to her strategic puzzle.

As part of her strategic review, she initiated an intense review of all the science projects in their research portfolio. Each of her projects took a system view and recognized the cutting-edge research in their field, the marketplace, and their competitors.

The portfolio review identified some projects to terminate and priority projects where they would focus their resources. Some of her projects were in areas that were mature and others that were new and at the start-up phase. Other areas of research needed to start new lines of research and move into fresh approaches. Mary and her team also recognized that there were some employee concerns that would have an impact on their engagement and motivation.

The gaps they identified would need to be filled if they were to achieve their strategic goals. These gaps formed part of her strategic plan, and she developed mid-range and long-range goals and measures in each area. Mary took a system view to understand her strategy and the context to achieve this strategy.

She also understood that, in her field of science, the external environment changed at a faster pace than before. New scientific advances in understanding cancer reshaped the approach to cancer treatment and the marketplace. She also knew that technology and social media redefined how people interact with each other. Just like the conditions that impacted the Nantucket whalers, she knew that she needed to define strategies that would make the most of her science.

The risk was that if she did not have plans that considered the changing environment, the organization and strategic goals would be left behind and become extinct. Mary had to convince her staff not to become complacent and not to believe that what made them successful in the past would ensure success for the future.

CHARLES S. DORMER

Chapter Summary

System thinking is of value in defining strategic plans. Analyzing the system in which you work is critical understanding the context for strategic plans. This thinking represents the framework leaders employ to develop strategic intent, strategic goals, and strategic plans.

System thinking is about analyzing and contemplating the whole, not individual parts. It also involves understanding how parts of a system interact and are interconnected to form the whole system.

I cannot overemphasize the need for strategic leaders to develop knowledge of both the internal environment and the external marketplace and competitors when developing strategic plans. This principle applies to organizations, products and projects, portfolios of assets, and individual strategies.

Leaders do not employ system thinking as much as they could. Analytical thinking has limitations; no matter how good the analysis of the parts of an organization, it may not predict the whole system. Fragmentation of the organization, either through organizational structure or by making changes in one part of a system, leads to the danger that the benefits of the whole system will be lost.

Organizations are systems in themselves, and great leaders analyze their organizations from design, characteristics, and conditions perspectives.

Five dimensions comprise an organization: talent and leadership behavior; skills, competencies, and technologies; culture and environment; organizational structure including matrices; and processes and decision-making. All five dimensions are involved in analyzing how people perform work in an organization. Changing an organization in a transformational way requires changing all five dimensions at the same time.

Organizational characteristics include the maturity of the organization. Characteristics in a start-up company or a well-established company, for example, display differences in maturity and complexity.

System thinking also considers a key characteristic: the organization's portfolio of assets and intellectual property. Leaders can use analysis of this portfolio, in the context of the external environment, marketplace, and competition, to prioritize the assets and focus resources on top-priority projects. Organizational conditions include engagement and motivation of employees, the impact of leadership styles, and the readiness for change.

As a strategic leader, if you conduct a system analysis or strategic-planning exercise, you should identify the current state and possible future states of the organization, product, portfolio, or yourself. The future-state analysis should focus on what is needed to deliver on strategic goals. From the analysis of the current state and the desired future state, you can formulate strategic plans to fill the gap.

System analysis and strategic plans should not be static; they should be flexible to enable adapting to dynamic changes in both internal and external environments. When defining the strategy for your organization and products, a system approach could help you shape the system rather than just reacting to business environmental changes.

Key Learnings about System Thinking

- Energetic, impactful leaders are system thinkers. They analyze the system of which they are a part, and they frame their strategic plans and actions in the context of the whole system, not individual parts.
- They understand their internal organization including structure, competencies, talent, processes, and culture.
- They understand their external environments and recognize patterns, trends, challenges, interconnections, and interactions with their system.
- They analyze the gap between their current state and a desired future state that is needed to deliver their strategic goals.

CHARLES S. DORMER

Action Plan for Improving System Thinking

In your action plan, take time to reflect on your strengths and your opportunity for growth. This self-reflection has two parts. First, review the following questions and rate yourself for a strength or an opportunity for growth for each question. Next, think about actions that you can take to enhance your strength or develop your opportunity for growth.

1. Do you actively seek data to understand your current system, both internal and external?
2. Do you look for patterns and trends to understand current state and desired future state?
3. Do you understand interconnections within your system?
4. How well do you know your organization's current design (talent, processes, competencies, structure, and culture)?
5. How well do you understand your company's maturity (a start-up or a well-established company)?
6. How well do you understand your organization's portfolio of assets, intellectual property, properties, and characteristics?
7. Do you understand what it takes to ensure your employees and colleagues are motivated and engaged?
8. How well do you assess your organization as being ready for change?
9. How well do you understand strategic gaps that need to be filled to deliver your strategic goals?

Chapter 4
Exploring Self-Wisdom: Inner Image

"This above all: to thine own self be true, And it must follow, as the night the day, Thou canst not be false to any other man."

William Shakespeare
(Hamlet)

How can you understand yourself as a leader? What are your tendencies when it comes to your leadership style? Do you know your strengths, weaknesses, emotions, and feelings? Do you understand the emotions of others, and are you empathetic to their thoughts and emotions? This is all part of self-wisdom. All effective leaders possess this wisdom. They use this wisdom so that they can maximize the creation of energy in others to deliver their strategy.

Here is another question that focuses on an important aspect of self-wisdom: Do you have a closed mindset (or viewpoint) that drives your assumptions, the way you act, and the way you learn and adapt from your experiences; or do you have an open mindset? Acquiring self-wisdom depends on self-reflection. Energizing, impactful leaders must possess a high level of empathy, knowing how others feel and what they need to be successful. They must develop an open mindset, which enables learning from experiences and changing as necessary rather than getting stuck in fixed ways of thinking.

Fortunately, self-wisdom can be developed. This chapter explores the importance of self-awareness, empathy, and mindset and shows you how to improve these qualities. These are large topics; so, please remember you are on a learning journey for improving your leadership effectiveness, which will last all your career and possibly the rest your life. This chapter helps you understand some of the potential roads that you may want to travel.

Why Self-Reflection is So Crucial to Success

Self-reflection is a critical skill for successful leadership to acquire self-wisdom. In self-reflection, you are thoughtful and aware of your inner state. You become mindful of how your experiences and biases shape your thoughts.

One way to increase self-awareness is through self-reflection, putting aside time to reflect on situations that demonstrate your strengths and your opportunities to grow. Self-awareness is extremely important for leaders because those thoughts, feelings, and biases drive their decision-making and actions. (A later chapter explores more fully the impact of emotions and biases on decision-making.)

Most of us are aware of extreme emotions or feelings that we experience such as anger, regret, or sadness. But even subtle feelings may trigger certain behaviors in any given situation. Being attuned to your feelings takes practice and involves time to explore.

Outcome Goals for Self-Reflection

Throughout my career, I observed outcomes resulting from self-reflection and self-wisdom. I believe three outcomes are the most important reasons to develop this critical skill: (1) You will know your leadership gaps; (2) it will enable you to maintain focus, and (3) it will build your self-confidence.

Self-Reflection Goal: Identifying Your Leadership Gaps

After you establish your purpose and strategy, you need to identify the leadership skills you need to lead the organization and deliver your strategy. I use the term "leadership skills" rather than "leadership style" in this context because no one style of leadership fits all situations. In fact, different styles may be needed depending on the challenges you may face as a leader.

Leadership skills may include the ability to communicate an inspirational vision that will motivate a group to go above and beyond their normal performance. In addition, a leader may need skills in creating a culture that is highly creative and innovative. Or a leader may need skill in leading a virtual team that never gets to meet each other, such as a field sales force spread across a wide geographic area.

Chapter 3 discussed how to perform system analysis and strategic planning to identify the current state and possible future state of an organization, product, or portfolio. The same principle applies to leadership skills. By being self-aware of your strengths and weaknesses and understanding yourself, you can identify areas of growth where you can improve your effectiveness. The skills needed for the future state you want to develop means that you need to aspire to an "desired" self that is different from your current self when it comes to leadership skills. Identifying gaps between your "current" self and the "desired" self requires a high degree of self-awareness.

Self-reflection does not stop when you identify the gaps, as your external environment continually changes. You need to continually develop and grow as a leader. Energizing, impactful leaders always have an ongoing, dynamic development plan and constantly adapt and grow. They do not stop learning and are agile in their leadership journey.

Self-Reflection Goal: Maintaining Your Focus

The second reason why it is important to have a high degree of self-awareness relates to focus. As a leader, you need self-control so you can turn your focus away from distractions that hinder achieving your goal. You also will find self-awareness and self-control invaluable in helping you recover from setbacks so you can move forward again.

I experienced the feeling of loss of self-control, and my experience may serve as a good example. My task was giving an especially important presentation to the board members of the company where I was employed. Like most people, I felt nervous. I made many presentations before; but, for some reason, this felt different. Within a few minutes of starting the presentation, I became aware of a feeling of fear and anxiety. My breath became short and my blood pressure rose. This was an unusual feeling for me, and I suddenly become aware of this. It took a few minutes for me to gain the cognitive control that I needed to complete the presentation successfully.

Following the presentation, I took some time to reflect on the situation. What was the feeling? What triggered the reaction? My reflection was that I had a strong sense of wanting to be successful in my presentation, and I feared I was not clear in my message. The basis for my fear was my not wanting to fail in front of this high-level group of board members and appear to not know what I talked about. I felt stressed in this situation.

This example illustrates another point to consider when thinking about self-awareness. External factors can influence your internal state of mind and your ability to be self-aware. The most obvious example is when you are under stress. The example of my presentation to the board shows that the acute stress induced by my fear and anxiety had an impact on my immediate feelings.

Chronic stress deeply affects your internal state of mind. Chronic stress raises your cortisol levels. Long-term "distress" can have some serious long-term effects including having a negative impact on your health and well-being. Under these conditions, you may even overuse your strengths and have a negative impact.

In coaching my clients, I see incidents of this effect. An example is a leader who is very driven and results oriented. This strength may have brought the leader a great deal of success; but under stress, the strength may be overused, causing the leader to become overly competitive and aggressive. In other words, in some situations, a strength can be valuable; but when under stress, it can be destructive and derailing.

Being self-aware of your level of stress is not as easy as it may seem. We know when we are overworked and feeling overwhelmed by a looming deadline or sudden influx of requests that are all urgent. Monitoring yourself for chronic stress is more difficult. You may know the story of the "boiling frog." If you put a frog into boiling water (not something I would suggest you do; apologies for the cruel image) it will, predictably, jump out. If you put the same frog into cold water and slowly increase the heat to the boiling point, the frog will not jump out but will succumb to the heat. I did not try this experiment myself, but it seems logical.

The point of the frog illustration: If you are in a high-stress situation, you will immediately be aware of the stress. But if the stress levels increase slowly over time, you may not be aware of the stress you are under until you start to see the negative impacts of chronic stress, such as health issues and inability to make good decisions.

At one point in my career, I experienced a lot of international travel and was proud of the fact that I did not suffer from jet lag. When I stopped travelling for a while, I realized that during my heavy travel period I suffered from jet lag all the time.

One of the impacts of feeling stress is that you can lose focus and become distracted by the overwhelming nature of stress. It is important that you remember that a critical part of being self-aware is monitoring your levels of stress and identifying how that impacts your behavior and distracts your focus on delivering your strategy.

Self-Reflection Goal: Self-Confidence

A third important reason for being self-aware relates to being self-confident. To be a successful leader, you need to be confident in your ability, know your strengths, and commit to a course of action. There will be many times when you will be tested as a leader, times when other people disagree with your ideas. When you know something is the right thing to do, you need self-confidence to stand up for what you believe. Being aware of your strengths will give you the confidence to trust your intuition.

Not all decisions and actions you take will be supported by a complete set of data to fully understand a particular situation. There will be times when it is appropriate to take a course of action that may have risks. For instance, if you challenge the status quo or introduce a new product or idea, you may feel uncomfortable with the uncertainty in a situation. Having self-confidence and trusting your intuition may be required to stay the course as you meet opposing views or resistance to your ideas.

An example from my coaching career is a client who was a senior leader in a large company. She advanced in the company by holding several roles of increasing responsibility as the company undertook a lot of change and restructuring over the years.

When I met this client, the company just finished another restructure of her division, and she had a third new boss in two years. She felt confused and vulnerable in her new role and perceived the new job as a backward step in her career. She had a new team and felt some resistance from the team toward her ideas. The impact of her situation: she lost self-confidence and often did not speak at meetings. She was concerned that she was too silent. She constantly replayed conversations in her head after the interactions were over. This habit had a still further negative impact on her confidence: she felt that she was a different person than in her early career when she was much more driven. She was also conscious that she thought and acted in a political way too often.

To deliver her strategy in her new role, she needed to energize her team and build her confidence. In my experience, this is not an unusual situation for people who become "gun shy" after many reorganizations. The impact can be that they become paralyzed and inactive, not sure of what is the right thing to do. They become risk averse.

The important first step with my client was identifying and reaffirming her strengths, the strengths that made her successful in the past. Through a process of making her more aware of her feelings and what triggered those feelings, it was possible to help her rebuild her confidence.

When considering self-confidence, a point that is equally important to being aware of your strengths is being aware of your weaknesses. It gives you a good understanding of your limitations. Of course, you can build your strengths and develop your weaknesses to overcome limitations; but you risk losing self-confidence if you overstep your areas of expertise and fail.

As an example, I am a leadership coach. I make it clear to the people I coach that I am not a marriage guidance counselor or psychiatrist and, if they need help in these areas, I am not an expert and refer them to someone else who could help them. If I tried to help in these areas, I would soon be out of my depth and would risk failing to help them. By working within the boundaries of my expertise, I can be confident in my ability. Hence, by recognizing my limitations, I am of greater help to my clients. Self-awareness of my strengths and limitations can focus my efforts towards being successful, and I can be self-confident in helping my clients.

The Impact of Self-Awareness

Throughout my career, I observed a quality shown by great strategic leaders: they can clearly demonstrate their strengths but also open themselves to be vulnerable by recognizing their weaknesses. By being slightly vulnerable, leaders appear more human, more authentic, and more trustworthy. This has two big impacts.

The first impact is that these leaders are more approachable and appear to be more open to feedback. Some leaders say to employees that they have an "open door" policy; but, in reality they may not be approachable, and employees may avoid interactions with them. The danger of not being approachable is that a leader may not be fully aware of developing issues in the organization. A later chapter discusses the importance of having a way of raising issues and managing conflict.

The second impact of leaders who show vulnerability is that it gives permission for employees to also display weaknesses. If the leader appears to be perfect, having no weaknesses, it is difficult for employees not to mirror that behavior. There is a big advantage for employees feeling able to display their weaknesses, as it is the first step to learning and developing those weaknesses into strengths.

Showing your vulnerable side takes a high degree of self-awareness and encourages self-awareness in your employees. By becoming aware of your weaknesses, you can be genuinely authentic—not just appear to be authentic, but really be your authentic self.

One of the major impacts of being self-aware is the ability to trust your intuition. This trust comes from being aware of your emotions that may be biased, based on your state of mind. An appreciation of shifts in your mindset is an important piece of self-awareness.

A good example of the negative impact of your state of mind is what happens if you carry residual emotions into an interaction. For example, you may be in a meeting that is highly emotional, and you discuss issues such as restructuring, about which you feel concerned and stressed. If you leave that meeting and move on to your next meeting, you may carry some of that residual emotion into your next meeting. We have all been in the situation where a leader rushes into a meeting late and, for reasons unrelated to the topic at hand, appears to be overly emotional. The leader probably brings the residual emotions from the prior meeting.

A best practice I use to overcome this effect is to build into my schedule ten minutes between meetings, so that I can re-center myself emotionally before going to the next meeting. One of the advantages of being aware of your feelings and emotions is that you could monitor this residual effect.

Another aspect of being self-aware is how you project your feelings and emotions to other people. You can be aware of this by monitoring the other person's reaction to you. A method I find useful is to take advantage of video conferences as well as face-to-face meetings. The advantage of video conferencing is that, as well as seeing the other people in the conference, you also get the opportunity to observe your own image. This means that you can monitor yourself and realize how you project your emotions and feelings. This obviously is in combination with knowing how you feel at that time.

Being aware of your difference from others is another aspect of self-awareness that deserves time for self-reflection. It is important to know who you are and where you came from. I spend time with my coaching clients discussing their career, background, experiences, and what influenced the way they frame the world. We also discuss some of the key decisions they made during their career as well as how and why they made them. Discovering this unique experience, skills, background, and way of thinking helps shape an understanding of their strengths and biases. This aspect of self-awareness has an impact on understanding how you make decisions and take actions.

The Critical Skill of Having Empathy

Are you empathetic toward other people's feelings? Having empathy is a necessary and important skill for effective leadership. The discussion here focuses on three benefits of developing and using empathy: it will help you in influencing situations, it will help you in being open to other people's ideas, and it will help you understand the impact of your decisions and actions.

Empathy Helps You in Influencing Situations

As a leader, you will need to manage teams to optimize their productivity. Influencing them to achieve your goal requires understanding their feelings about the work, the other team members, and even you as their leader. Another influencing situation is that you may need to coach employees who are about to experience organizational change. Employees care about the work they do. Your effectiveness at driving change will depend on your recognizing their feelings about the status quo and the change. Or you may be in an executive leadership meeting where you need to understand your colleagues' feelings so you can influence their commitment to a goal. Emotional empathy is necessary for your effectiveness in such influencing situations.

A crucial ability in being an energizing, impactful leader is motivating your team, followers, or employees to commit to the strategic goal and plan you want to achieve. It is common in many organizations trying to drive change that people appear to agree to the change, but they do not commit to the change. They prefer the status quo. Often, they exhibit passive-aggressive behaviors that can cause costly delays or even sabotage the desired outcome. Gaining real commitment to follow you in strategic goals and plans requires empathy that enables you to understand their true feelings.

Your primary role as a leader is to deliver on a strategy and fulfill a strategic vision that is important to an organization. In most cases, this involves getting people to follow you. This necessitates balancing between the vision and the ultimate success versus the delivery of required actions and activities. Your followers may not want to deliver those actions. When you are empathetic, you understand how they feel in the context of delivering on the strategic vision and plans. But you must avoid giving people what they want at the cost of delivering the organization's goals. Alternatively, delivering the organization's goals at the cost of how people feel and providing them what they need can result in short-term gains at the expense of longer-term sustainability of the organization. As a leader, you should be aware of this necessary balance.

Empathy Opens You to Other People's Ideas

Energizing, impactful leaders are open to other people's ideas. This does not happen unless the leader is empathetic and wants to understand other perspectives and the way other people frame a problem.

In my experience, being open to new views and ideas adds to the quality of your thinking. For example, I am acutely aware that I have a set of biases that makes me feel a particular way regarding a situation. These biases are based on my experience in life and my upbringing and background. My experience regarding such factors as culture, gender, race, nationality, religion, class, and age frames my perspective, understanding, and feelings in a particular situation. These factors shape the lens with which I view the world.

There is an advantage to having a strong set of values: it helps me to make sense of a complex and somewhat chaotic world. The disadvantage is that these biases may close opportunities to view a problem with a different lens. The classic illustration of viewing a portion of an elephant's body from only your point of view limits your ability to see the whole picture and that it is an elephant. If all you see is the elephant's trunk, you might mistake it for a snake.

Trying to understand other people's perspectives and putting yourself in other people's shoes will open you to diverse points of view. In other words, trying to understand how people view a situation when using a different lens gives you a different view.

Empathy Helps You Understand The Impact of Your Decisions and Actions

Becoming an effective leader means you need to understand the impact of your decisions and actions and ensure you create positive energy. You cannot understand the impact unless you seek to understand others' perspectives. If you lack a good sense of seeing a problem from multiple viewpoints, you risk making decisions and taking actions that have unintended consequences.

As a leader, you cannot be an expert in everything and, from your vantage point, you cannot see all the possible impacts of a decision or action. This is particularly true when considering transformational change. To deliver on your strategic goals, you may embark on a major transformation of your organization. As you think about the possible options and potential changes that you need to make to your organization, it is important that you get input from a wide range of people so you can consider all possible perspectives. This will enable you to maximize the probability of success of your changes in delivering the results you need.

My experience is that a leader in a situation of transformational change often feels alone. Usually, the leader cannot share details with a wide group of people ahead of the transformation. There may be constraints around confidentiality, particularly if the changes could have an impact on stock price and other sensitive matters. This situation can lead to a leader feeling isolated, which can be highly stressful. Isolation and stress can lead to poor decision-making. This can be a common experience, particularly if the leader feels he or she cannot show weakness or vulnerability.

Being a leader can be lonely. It is critical that you take advantage of understanding other people's perspectives and viewpoints. It is not just an academic exercise; it has an important impact on how you view problems, identify solutions, and implement decisions and actions.

Seeking other people's ideas and viewpoints can be as simple as getting to know the people in your organization. Learn about their backgrounds, their experiences. Try to understand how they see the world. My experience is that when you are genuinely interested in others (of course, with appropriate boundaries) you can really get to understand and value different perspectives. Putting yourself in someone else's shoes to look at a problem from that person's perspective can be a liberating and creative experience.

Being aware of how people around you feel and how they emotionally react to your decisions and actions can be the difference between being successful or unsuccessful in achieving your strategic goals.

Our emotions and feelings can significantly impact the level of energy we have toward a goal or a particular situation. If we feel "good" about the situation, we will have positive energy, feel motivated, and be engaged. If we feel "bad" about it, it creates negative energy, work becomes hard, and we lose motivation and become disengaged. For example, if you are afraid of a boss who is unpredictable and a bully, you will avoid interactions with that person and possibly find another job to get away from the situation.

Over the years, I learned that the best way to find out how people feel about a particular situation is to ask them. A simple question to an employee such as "How does this make you feel?" will open new conversations and a deeper connection between you and your employee. It may also bring new insights into the consequences of your decisions and actions.

In business, the changing nature of the environment means that leaders make decisions that affect employees and other people associated with an organization. Maintaining the status quo is not an option in a dynamic and fast-changing business. Therefore, it is inevitable that some of your decisions will cause pain, even if they are best for the business or your organization.

However, I would argue that you do not need to cause long-term, sustained pain. As a leader, you can minimize suffering of those affected by the pain of a decision by being transparent, caring, and understanding their feelings. This behavior, combined with treating people with respect and dignity, can take the suffering out of pain caused by uncertainty or changing status quo and taking people out of their comfort zone. I believe that the single biggest impact of understanding others' feelings is to be aware of when you cause suffering to people in your care.

Another important aspect in understanding how someone else feels is using your senses to measure the temperature of your organization. Being sensitive to the feelings of individuals, groups, and teams comes from regular interactions with people in your organization. This ability to sense feelings varies widely from leader to leader but also varies by the nature of your interactions. For most of us, face-to-face interactions are the most sensitive way to pick up on emotions and feelings of other people in the interaction. Face-to-face interactions display subtle physical signs of emotions and body language. These signs may be incongruent with what the individual says.

As a leader, I found that "walking the job" is the best way to pick up on the feelings of the organization. For example, each morning I went into the lab to get a sense of the temperature of the team that day. It was easy to pick up indications that there was something on their minds. The advantage of this approach is that you can address the issue there and then. By "walking the job," you can also sense when people feel off their game. They may be sick or have a personal issue that distracts them. There is a big advantage to showing your employees that you truly care about their situation and that you are not engaged in a cynical, manipulation but, rather, that you have an authentic concern for your staff.

You cannot address issues and concerns if your staff members do not feel comfortable in raising them. The risk is that something you are not aware of as a small problem may come back to bite you as a big issue. I will discuss the importance of listening in the next chapter. Remember that understanding others' feelings starts with being sensitive and is enhanced by asking questions and truly listening.

Face-to-face interactions are the most sensitive way to pick up on people's feelings and emotions; however, in today's virtual world, people may work in remote locations. I find video conferencing also useful in picking up on subtle body language and identifying incongruence between what someone says, and the signals sent through the person's body language. Video also has the added advantage of your being able to monitor your own body language. The third best option is to pick up the phone, have a conversation and pick up cues by asking questions.

The least satisfactory way of picking up on somebody's feelings and emotions is through email. In my experience, very few people can express subtle emotions through email and social media, even with the use of capital letters and emojis. You can avoid confusion and wasting time by having a phone conversation or a video call rather than initiating a long stream of emails.

Having a good sense of other people's feelings is an important skill for a strategic leader to hone. It can have a positive impact on creating energy, motivation, engagement, and productivity. This is also important in understanding team dynamics, which I discuss more fully in a later chapter.

Minimizing Employees' Unhappiness. As mentioned above, giving people what they need to reach their strategic goal is distinct from giving them just what they want. There is no doubt that people that are happy are more productive and can be energized, engaged, and motivated. One could argue that making employees happy is not the primary goal of a leader. But the leader can go a long way to minimize unhappiness, and you will want to do this because it helps you motivate employees to be more productive. As a leader, you want to ensure your employees have positive feelings about their job, their purpose, and the future of the company and their jobs.

As I mentioned earlier, as a leader, you need to provide what people need rather than what they want. There are some points that are worth considering here, particularly in respect to the feelings of meaning, purpose, interest, pride, and inspiration; after all, these factors lead to happiness. As an effective leader, you can inspire employees with meaning and purpose and generate a feeling of interest and pride around the organization's mission. For most employees, your generating these feelings goes beyond what they want. It is what they need to stay motivated, engaged, happy, and more productive.

How Your Mindset Affects Your Success as a Leader

Another element that is critical in your ability to understand yourself is your mindset. In my coaching practice, I find that one of the most important things to investigate with my clients is how their mindset can be a barrier to their being effective.

A mindset is a mental attitude. It can influence your willingness to be flexible. Or it can be an obstacle to change. It is a big factor in what you believe about yourself and about other people, so it affects how you interact with others. It affects how you take on new situations. Or it may cause you to get trapped in the past. Basically, it is a huge governing factor in how you think and behave.

Your mindset is a crucial factor in your success as a leader because it influences your decisions and your leadership behaviors. I cannot overstress how important it is to understand your mindset and identify your thoughts and feelings that arise from it.

Your longstanding beliefs and emotional feelings influence either a "closed" mindset or an "open" mindset. People with a closed mindset often believe that things cannot be changed. It is not unusual for them to hesitate or resist situations where they perceive they have a weakness that they believe cannot be overcome. They do not adapt well to change and often resist it. They seek to preserve the status quo. They feel uncomfortable with change and feel that they must prove themselves and their value. They often do not listen when others talk.

Leaders with a closed mindset often behave in an authoritarian manner to get employees to work in a manner that aligns with the leader's beliefs about employees' roles and responsibilities.

Furthermore, having a closed mindset can lead to not wanting to take risk. In fact, trying something new may lead to people losing their current status.

In contrast, those with an open mindset typically are open to change and believe that they can adapt and learn to do things better. People with an open mindset are good at brainstorming ideas, look for innovation, have future-oriented thoughts, love to learn, focus on opportunities for growth, and are willing to change. People with an open mindset are willing to take risks and view change is an opportunity to try something new and learn new skills.

I coach my clients to determine in which areas they have a closed or open mindset. I ask, for instance, "Do you make room for options or new ideas?" "Are you open to learning new ways when you experience failure or a setback?" "Are you willing to seek feedback from others and change?" "Are you willing to gain insight from others as to opportunities for growth?" "Are you open to trying to learn others' perspectives?"

Feedback from others can help you validate or disprove your insights. Awareness of your strengths, weaknesses, and tendencies is critical to managing your mindset with a goal of improving your leadership skills.

Examples of How a Leader's Mindset Affects Interactions and Outcomes

Consider how a leader's closed mindset affects others as the leader focuses on protecting his or her self-image. Such a leader feels special and often talks even without having something meaningful to say. The leader also does not listen when others talk. A meeting with this kind of leader frustrates other participants who may be more introverted in nature. They do not get a word in edgewise and may conclude that they do not contribute enough.

Another example is leaders whose mindset makes them feel they are more special than others. They tend to overestimate their strengths and may even believe they cannot improve themselves. They also tend to judge others. This kind of behavior risks closing opportunities to learn valuable insights from others.

A third example is how a mindset affects the outcome of change. Leaders with open mindsets have an ability to come back from setbacks. They are resilient and still manage to pursue goals despite setbacks and other challenges. In contrast, those with closed mindsets fear others' opinions of them if there is a failure. They fear criticism or losing a positive opinion and think a setback will define their leadership capability going forward.

Leaders with an open mindset often view a setback as a call to action for increasing their focus on achieving goals. They ask what they can do differently in the future. This type of leader performs "post-mortems" on both successful and unsuccessful efforts to learn lessons and keep improving their performance.

As I pointed out earlier, a mindset can be a barrier to success as a leader. For example, someone with a closed mindset may not want to risk failure and will not be open to learning new ways of doing things and learning from successes and failures.

Ask yourself if you are more afraid of losing your current success or more excited by opportunities to be challenged and grow. If you are more afraid of losing your current success, or at least the perception of success, you will be less likely to reach your full potential. You need to be open to feedback and be comfortable showing vulnerability.

I see leaders who play organizational politics to a degree that causes others not to see them as authentic or trustworthy. These leaders often use politics to hang on to the power and influence they have rather than look for opportunities to be more influential. With their closed mindset, they focus on preserving the status quo because they think they will lose by changing it. But, as I explained earlier, leaders need to challenge the status quo if they want to achieve their visionary strategic goals.

Successful leaders also want to continually learn. In my experience, the ability to learn is one of the most critical skills in a leader's armory. Learning is at the heart of understanding yourself as a leader and knowing how to be effective. Developing as a leader and filling your "leadership gaps" requires that you have an open mindset.

A final example, and a barrier to leadership success, is how a closed mindset relates to one's attitude about entitlement. I explained entitlement earlier as feeling more special than other people. Leaders with a closed mindset often think they are entitled to not changing but others must change.

A feeling of entitlement affects how one deals with problems. People who feel entitled often exit from a problem situation rather than undertaking change to solve the problem. Exaggerated feelings can have a significant negative impact on a leader's engagement, mood, and happiness. Negative impacts can significantly affect the leader's level of stress and the way the leader behaves while under stress. To succeed as an effective strategic leader, you need to create positive energy in your staff and in yourself.

The difference between a closed and open mindset is an important distinction. As a strategic leader in a fast, dynamic, changing environment, it is important to be open to growth, challenge yourself, and have a desire to learn. Equally as important is your ability to bounce back from setbacks and see failures as opportunities to learn. Being conscious of your mindset is critical to developing your ability to lead others to achieve your strategic goals.

You probably know of the Peter Principle, the well-known advice about decline and people rising to their level of incompetence. I use the principle as a warning that leaders with a closed mindset may be promoted but eventually will reach their level of incompetence if they do not grow and learn along the way.

I also warn that it is common to give young leaders increasing responsibility without the help they need to develop the leadership skills needed to take on new roles. Under those conditions, leaders risk being victims of the Peter Principle and their growth being blocked.

I think that leadership in a dynamic environment often feels like leaders walking up an escalator that goes down. If the leaders stand still, they will go backwards and eventually fall off the bottom if they are not careful. Having an open mindset, challenging yourself, and learning from experience will keep you moving upwards.

CHARLES S. DORMER

Energizing, Impactful Leadership in Action: Developing Self-Wisdom

Greg was of one of those children that always have great ideas and can sell their ideas to anyone who listens. In college, he started a company developing customized software for his classmates to help him study and revise more effectively. At business school, his classmates saw him as the archetypal entrepreneur.

Upon graduating, he joined a professor in launching a biotech company. The professor discovered a gene that regulates glucose metabolism and thought it was a product that could be developed for rare diseases that affect a small group of children but also could potentially have wider use in diabetes patients. As CEO, Greg used his skills to effectively attract venture capitalists to the company and soon achieved a second and third round of funding.

Greg encountered significant challenges as his company grew. He had to transition from being the CEO of the small entrepreneurial company, where people wore many hats, to being a CEO of a mid-size company. As the company grew, so did the need for managerial processes, company-wide policies, and standardized HR practices. As the science advanced, the company faced a need for standard operating procedures and regulatory compliance. These changes dictated that Greg create a different organizational culture to be successful.

In the fast-paced entrepreneurial culture of Greg's start-up company, working in a somewhat chaotic way was acceptable. But the culture in the growing mid-size company changed to become more bureaucratic and emphasize standardized processes and policies in a heavily regulated industry. Greg struggled with this new environment and soon realized he did not know all the answers. He brought in experts and trusted them to make the right decisions. He could no longer be directly involved in everything.

Things came to a head for Greg as he arrived at his office one morning at his usual time at 7:30 a.m. The HR director met him before he started his usual busy schedule of meetings and explained that there was a sexual harassment complaint by a young female employee involving one of the senior team.

This was not the first time for rumors about this type of behavior in the male-dominated company. Greg knew they needed to act quickly. By that evening, he felt comfortable that a plan was in place to work through the issue. He also committed to investigate how he could be a better leader; he knew that the firm would only be successful if he could transition to leading this growing company.

Greg was concerned about his company's culture that led to biases. He knew a cultural change had to be led from the top, and he committed to lead the change. The HR Director suggested that Greg use Josephine, a seasoned executive coach with a lot of business experience in corporate life before setting up a coaching business.

Josephine started by gathering background through asking questions about Greg's career history. She also performed a psychometric analysis and a 360-degree feedback exercise for Greg. She carried out confidential interviews with some of Greg's board members and his direct reports. After gathering the data from these analyses, she arranged to meet with Greg to review the results. The aim of this session was to increase Greg's level of self-awareness.

According to Greg's input in the 360-degree assessment, he was a "people person," and his staff really enjoyed working with him. He was naturally very friendly with everyone and understood people. He had an instinct for knowing how people feel about a situation. Although he was always busy, he found time to get feedback from the staff and was open to their ideas. He liked to empower his staff to make decisions. He also had a great family support network and enjoyed time with his wife and son.

The psychometric assessment showed Greg's dominant leadership style was directive, meaning he tended to tell people what to do. This style was a strength for him in the past and resulted in his being results oriented and getting things done. The assessment also showed that when he was under stress the style became more exaggerated.

Reflecting on the data, Greg realized that he would need to

supplement the directive style with other styles that would get the most out of his talented staff in achieving his strategic goals. To change the culture of his organization, he would need everyone on board and committed to doing things differently.

The data from the 360-degree feedback was a wake-up call for Greg. His staff expressed the view that he was too directive, which made him unapproachable at times, particularly when he was busy. His staff appreciated his strengths and commitment to getting results. However, they said he often did not take time to ask people's opinions and get their ideas. The view of most of Greg's staff was that he was not a good listener. Contrary to his beliefs, most of his staff did not see him as a people person and said he was often unaware of how his staff felt about his decisions. Some of the staff expressed the view that he did not ask for feedback. They expressed the thought that this 360-degree assessment was the first time Greg asked for their views on his leadership. They appreciated being asked and were happy to give their feedback.

Greg learned a lot of information from the session with Josephine. He recognized that he had an opportunity to become more self-aware of his leadership style. There was some good feedback that would help him to be aware of his strengths and identify areas that he could develop to become even more effective as a leader. The self-reflection journey for Greg took some time before he could fully accept the feedback; but in doing so, he knew he had a great opportunity to learn from the feedback.

He initially focused on understanding why and when he could be unapproachable. He needed to be self-aware of the behaviors that led him to not being as open as he wanted to be with his employees. He reflected on times that he felt he did not want to be approached by staff and when he was less open to listening to their opinions and ideas. He had a good idea when this occurred; it was when he felt stressed and under tight deadlines.

The experience with the coach was valuable, as she helped him realize the cycle of behavior that sent him into a negative loop: stress leading to distractions, leading to more stress, leading to being less approachable, leading to not asking for help, leading to more stress, leading to not being open to learning, and on and on. His primary focus now was to find ways to reverse this cycle.

Greg realized that developing his skills and being more empathetic were clear opportunities for his growth. To achieve his strategic goals in growing his company, he needed to develop ways to build his skills in understanding others. He began finding ways he could understand other people's perspectives. Even when he was busy, he would seek the opinions of others and be open to listening to their ideas. This change in behavior started with the way he interacted with the staff and the way he managed meetings.

He also started to be conscious of how people felt about a given situation. He implemented regular check-in meetings with his team to sense the temperature of the staff's feelings and emotions. His interactions with his staff became more open, honest, and more productive. He had the feeling that his group was more energized and engaged.

Greg also recognized that sometimes he had a closed mindset and was prone to think that he had something to prove. He also thought of himself as superior to others. He knew that his closed mindset led to stress between him and some members of his board. Greg started recognizing the triggers that led to his closed mindset. Working with his coach, Greg committed to shifting his mindset when he felt these triggers, shifting from a closed mindset into an open mindset. Being aware of his closed mindset was the first step. As Greg started making some changes in his behavior, he saw an impact on his stress levels and an increase in his team's productivity. He was on a journey to really understand what his staff needed to be the most productive they could be. He was clear about the purpose and mission of the company, and he shared success stories with everyone. Greg felt that there was an increase in energy, engagement, and pride in his staff around their mission to get the drugs to patients.

Greg knew that he was at the start of his journey to be more empathetic, but even his early progress made a big impact. He saw the return on investment for changing his behavior. He knew he had more work to do but was off to a great start.

Chapter Summary

This chapter explains the importance of self-reflection to increase your degree of self-wisdom, that is, knowing your strengths, weaknesses, emotions, and feelings. It is also important to understand your level of empathy, that is, understanding other people's perspectives, knowing how others feel, and sensing what they need.

Another focus of this chapter is the need to become aware of the leadership style you need to deliver your strategic goals. This self-awareness helps you identify your leadership gaps, which then become an opportunity for growth and enhancing your strengths.

It is important to maintain focus and not become distracted. It is also important to build self-confidence. Further, effective leadership necessitates exposing vulnerability so you can build trust, be approachable, trust your instincts, and dare to be different.

Another highlight is the importance of understanding your mindset and its impact on your biases, decision-making, and actions. There are advantages of an open mindset and barriers to success from a closed mindset. Your mindset impacts your self-image (feelings of entitlement and superiority), whether you overcome setbacks and build resilience, and whether you are open to learning.

Another critical skill for strategic leaders is being open to feedback. And it is important that you learn to grow as a leader so you can avoid being promoted to your level of incompetence.

Key Learnings About Self-Wisdom

- Energizing, impactful leaders are self-aware, empathetic, and have an open mindset. They know their strengths and weaknesses. Importantly, they can identify their emotions and feelings.
- They have a high level of self-control. They focus on their goals and not becoming distracted.
- They are self-confident and recognize their limitations.
- They are empathetic to others. They seek to understand other

people's perspectives. They empathize with what others feel and have a good sense of what others need.
- They have an open mindset. This mindset leads to a desire to learn (and learn from criticism), embrace challenges, and have a greater sense of free will.

Action Plan for Developing Self-Wisdom

In your action plan, take time to reflect on your strengths and your opportunity for growth. This self-reflection has two parts. First, review the following questions and rate yourself for a strength or an opportunity for growth for each question. Next, think about actions that you can take to enhance your strength or develop your opportunity for growth.

1. How aware are you? Do you know your strengths and weaknesses, your expertise, and your limitations? Are you in touch with how you feel at any given time and the emotions you feel?
2. Do you have a high level of self-control, stay calm in a crisis, and rebound from setbacks?
3. Do you have a high degree of focus? Can you pursue goals without distractions?
4. Are you approachable? Do you sometimes show vulnerability?
5. Do you understand others' perspectives? Can you put yourself "in other people's shoes?"
6. Do you have a strong capability for picking up on how others feel?
7. Do you have a good sense of what others need from you rather than just what they want?
8. Do you recognize the triggers that lead you to a closed or open mindset?
9. Are you open to learning from your successes and failures?
10. Do you seek feedback from others and then act upon it?

Chapter 5
Signaling to Others: Positive Presence

"We have two ears and one mouth so that we can listen twice as much as we speak."

Epictetus
(Ancient Greek philosopher)

To achieve your purpose and strategic goals, you need to create energy in others and influence them to follow you. Followers may be your team members, stakeholders, more senior management, investors, peers, or collaborators (internal and external). It may be that you have an idea you would like others to support. Or perhaps you want to convince your boss to agree with your views. As the leader, you need to influence others to respond the way you want so you can change courses of action.

How does influencing happen? Influencing others starts by changing yourself. To influence and elicit a different response from others, you could spend a lot of time and effort trying to change other people. but, ultimately, you can succeed only at changing yourself. In this chapter, you will learn how to change yourself so that you can have a positive impact on others.

Successful leaders influence others to follow their purpose and strategic goals through what I refer to as their "positive presence." Your positive presence includes being aware; managing and aligning communication of content; intentionally managing how others view you; and behaving in a way that fosters passion, trust, authenticity, and openness. Positive presence gives you the ability to make others feel comfortable and confident but challenged while delivering on your strategic goals.

I use the word "positive" because you influence by creating positive energy in other people. Positive influence is not about tricking or manipulating people; it is grounded in ethical leadership. I use the word "presence" in a broad sense referring to the way you present yourself to others in all your interactions, whether it is through face to face, video, telephone, or written communication.

I worked with great leaders in my career who create positive energy and influence others to follow their purpose and strategic goals, independent of whether they have direct control in a reporting relationship with the follower. These leaders achieve this by managing and monitoring their positive presence. Managing positive presence, in my view, is not just a "nice to have" skill; it is critical set of skills for energizing, impactful leaders.

In my experience, leaders with positive presence excel in three areas: content of their communication, their visibility, and leadership behaviors and skills.

Positive Presence Component: Content of Your Communications

An important component of positive presence is how and what you communicate with others. Leaders with a positive presence intentionally communicate with contextual vision, alignment, and credibility. Energizing, impactful leaders tend to be strategic and system thinkers. They often focus their communications on strategy—seeing the big picture and clearly articulating their vision and purpose. They create energy by inspiring others to follow; they accomplish this inspiration by having a compelling purpose that resonates with the people they want to follow them.

They also tend to have a wider context view and communicate with a wider system in mind than their area of expertise. This is sometimes referred to as "enterprise thinking." Enterprise leaders have the whole business in mind when making decisions and not just their immediate area of responsibility. When they communicate, they keep in mind their whole business or their whole industry.

Communication and projecting a positive presence can be complicated due to the many methods of communication (email, video conferencing, face-to-face meetings, blogs, social media posts, and other forms of electronic postings). An additional challenge arises when working with diverse and global teams where there are many opportunities to be misunderstood.

The important point for you to keep in mind regarding communication is to be intentional. Plan your communications so that you project a positive presence. From a leadership perspective, your communication style can have an impact on four important outcomes of positive presence: authenticity, building trust, being present in the moment for others, and influencing others. (These four outcomes will be discussed in more detail later in this chapter.)

Communication is a two-way street; there is the person communicating and the person receiving the communication. The perception others have of your positive presence is a result of your style as both a transmitter of the communication message and as the receiver of a message. The aim of effective communication is to be clear, concise, and understood by the receiver of the messages you communicate; so, it is important that you seek to understand whether the receiver of your message understood it as you intended. It is a good idea to ask questions of the recipient or summarize for clarity.

One of the most important skills for a leader is the ability to receive a message that involves being a great listener. (Listening will be discussed in greater detail later in this chapter.)

Part of being intentional in your communications is knowing your audience, those who receive your message. Consider the level of knowledge each member of your audience has around a subject and their style of receiving messages.

As an example of the importance of knowing your audience, imagine that you communicate through a presentation to a senior leadership group.

The objective of your presentation is to get their buy-in to your strategy and get a decision to provide resources. Some members of your audience may have some knowledge of the subject but only at a strategic level. Some of the audience may have a decision-making style that requires them to understand your proposal in great detail, while others just need the topline messages to make a decision. It may require that you meet with the senior leaders one on one or provide them a written document with the details they need so that they can feel comfortable making a decision.

When thinking about your audience, you should consider other questions. What is your relationship with your audience? Do you have a longstanding relationship, or are they new to you? What is your level of credibility with the audience? Do they view you as trustworthy or an expert in your technical field? Do you have a history of successful or unsuccessful communication with them? Do they prefer verbal or written communications? Understanding your audience for any communication is a first step to attaining your objective from the communication.

Another aspect of communication to how you present your story, whether it is in written form or verbal communication. I use the word "story" because great communicators capture the attention of their readers or audience by telling a compelling story whose narrative resonates with the receivers of the message in a way that motivates them to keep reading or listening. This is a skill that differentiates people who can gain trust, be authentic, and influence others.

In science, it is easy to fall into the trap of presenting "dry data," often with too much information and, in the case of presentations, too much crammed onto one PowerPoint slide. You need to lead your audience through the story that emerges from the data and lead them to exciting next steps and new experiments. A well-crafted presentation or written communication helps the audience come to an appreciation of the story line and builds excitement about wanting to see the next chapter.

Using humor in written communications or presentations can ease the tension of a dry presentation or written article. Although there is an advantage to using humor, there are also some dangers. Obviously, inappropriate humor does not have a place in most communications, but also there is a danger that the audience may misunderstand humor. This is particularly true with sarcasm that may not be appreciated in the same way across different cultures. Humor can also be misinterpreted based on the media you use. Face-to-face communication or video conferencing is safest, as you can see the reaction of the receivers of the humor. It is more difficult over the phone and through email. Although some well-placed wit can add to your positive presence, be careful using humor, as it can easily backfire. In this case, it is always best to be safe rather than sorry.

What about communication in meetings? In my coaching practice, I come across a question quite often: "How much is the right amount to contribute?" This is particularly true in science, as scientists tend to be introverted in nature and often feel they are not vocal enough. Keep in mind that it is the quality of your contribution that matters rather than the quantity of input. By quality, I mean well-thought-out appropriate comments that add to the discussion and add to your positive presence rather than speaking for the sake of being visible.

You may work with people who like the sound of their own voice or have something to say about everything, even if it is not relevant or insightful. It is my experience that others do not always view favorably someone who speaks for the sake of speaking. On the other hand, if you have a contribution but say nothing, others may view this negatively.

My advice is to make appropriate comments when they add to the discussion or move the discussion forward. There is a lot to be said by saying the right things at the right time. Your presence will be appreciated by what you say, not by how much airtime you use. If you are in a leadership position in a meeting, it does not mean you should dominate the discussion. Great leaders know when to talk and when to give others room to express themselves. Always default to the practice of being inclusive and creating an environment that lets everyone feel comfortable to contribute. (You will learn more about this practice in the next chapter.)

Positive Presence Component: Visibility

The second factor of positive presence is how you present yourself and are visible to others. Energizing, impactful leaders have several characteristics that dictate how people perceive them in the way they interact including self-confidence, passion, ease and comfort, and likeability. These characteristics result in a sense that the leader is in control even in difficult and challenging situations. They appear to project self-confidence, but not in an arrogant way.

There is a balance to strike here. Some people view over-confidence as being arrogant, and arrogance can cause a negative impact on others. They may become more reserved when confronted with someone perceived as arrogant.

Being self-confident comes from a high level of self-awareness and belief that you can be part of an interaction and want to be in the situation. Your body language and the voice you use help to express your confidence, even when not physically present.

In addition to displaying confidence, effective leaders are at ease and are comfortable even when put in a stressful situation or when they are challenged. Being at ease helps to foster confidence in what you discuss with your audience. People often perceive your comfort level as meaning you are emotionally centered and not appearing stressed by the situation. This may not always be the case and learning to "fake it" when you are nervous or stressed is a valuable skill to develop.

Positive presence also comes from your visual brand, which includes your body language, posture, and how you dress. Dress appropriately (professional business, business casual, or casual) for the audience with which you interact. I attended an industry conference where it was not surprising that there was almost a uniform, and it was clear with some participants' attire which company was their employer.

Some dress codes are more formal, whereas others are less formal. Dress code is part of organizational culture. There can be many influences on dress code such as geographical locations or type of profession. People in the business part of a company, particularly those who deal with customers, may wear a suit and tie in the case of men and more formal dress for women. In other cases (those in research and development, for example), dress code tends to be less formal. If there is a disconnect between your attire and the expectations of the audience, this can have a negative impact on your presence.

Posture is another aspect of your visual brand, even on video conferencing calls. I coached a senior leader who constantly looked at his computer during meetings. Other people perceived his behavior as hiding behind his laptop, and it had an impact on their perception of his confidence and comfort level in the meeting.

Energizing, impactful leaders have a positive impact on their presence by passionate enthusiasm. People who are passionate in the way they talk and behave help to create energy in others. It is difficult for others to feel excited by your idea if you are not enthusiastic about it.

You can also influence more people if they perceive you as likable. This is not a new idea, and Dale Carnegie identified this factor in his classic book, *How to Win Friends and Influence People*. Most of us tend to like people who are appropriately fun, optimistic, and positive in their mood and attitude. In my experience, effective leaders intentionally manage their visibility with self-confidence, comfort level, enthusiasm, and likeability.

Positive Presence Component: Leadership Behaviors and Skills

The third component of positive presence involves leaders behaving and having skills that result in a positive impact on others. To have a positive presence that encourages others to deliver on your purpose and strategies, I believe you should strive for the following five outcomes. (1) Have trust-filled relationships. (2) Be viewed as authentic. (3) Be perceived as being present in the moment and not distracted. (4) Have good interactions that involve effective listening. (5) Make appropriate use of influence and power dynamics.

CHARLES S. DORMER

Skills and Behaviors for Trust-Filled Relationships

People are more influenced by people they trust, and effective leaders act intentionally to create energy and develop followers by engendering trust. If people do not trust you, it is more difficult for them to believe you and be motivated and engaged for your mission and strategic goals. Building trust and trust-based organizations is not just about providing a nice place to work, although that is important because we spend so much time at work.

Your trustworthiness also has an impact on your organization's productivity. When employees do not trust their leaders, the result is failure in achieving strategic goals. It is a domino effect: mistrust leads to unhappiness and stress, which causes the employees to become less engaged, which then leads to low energy and decreased productivity. This is a recipe for high staff turnover, especially the top talent. (In my experience, the top talent leaves first.)

At a recent workshop of management consultants looking at success factors in strategic relationships, I asked, "What are some of the characteristics that build trust, which you look for in a partner?" Their responses included sharing fresh insights, anticipating problems, no surprises when working with them, owning mistakes, being predictable, active listening, willingness to understand others' point of view, demonstrating advocacy for others, being a learner, and demonstrating trust behaviors.

I also asked the group, "What are some ways to build trust?" Their answers: communication (face to face in the first instance), living up to commitments, following up, transparency, giving back, being consistent in actions and product delivery, taking risks and managing risk, managing ego, and sharing values.

As an energizing, impactful leader, several other behaviors increase your ability to build trust. These represent your outer core and can be judged best by others rather than yourself. These include the following: being authentic, being consistently open and honest in your interactions, being willing to make commitments and living up to them and being present in the moment.

Other behaviors that engender trust in others include being willing to actively listen and learn (having an open mindset), being empathetic to others, being self-aware, and being open to giving and receiving feedback.

Building trust is key to your success, and you need to intentionally manage and build trust-filled relationships. The aim of managing a positive presence is to build relationships and trust. The outcome is that your employees and partners are more engaged, happier, and more productive. You need to manage your positive presence actively to create positive energy and minimize the impact of negative energy in your organization and collaborations. You should direct this positive energy at delivering on your mission and strategy.

Skills and Behaviors for Authenticity

Another dimension of positive presence is authenticity or being authentic, in other words, real and not pretentious. If you lack authenticity, your followers will perceive you are not honest, or if you lack integrity. They may even perceive you as manipulative.

How do people judge authenticity? Employees look for indicators such as discrepancies between what the leader says and what the leader does or behaving one way around some people but behaving a different way around others (not being genuine).

In my experience, there are several themes around being authentic. For example, authentic leaders have a desire to invest in leadership behaviors and develop themselves, which arises from their open mindset. They are self-aware rather than being a passive observer of their life. Authentic leaders also are open to feedback from others. They are open to learning and reframing setbacks as opportunities to grow.

Authenticity comes from your inner core—your values, true personality, spirit, and character. These aspects are visible to others through your decisions and actions. It also comes from how you manage yourself as perceived by others. It is your ability to manage your emotions and feelings, even when under stress. It is difficult for others to perceive your true authentic self if you let your emotions get the better of you.

Your true self will be demonstrated in different ways based on your audience, but if you possess authenticity, you will not change your inner core to accommodate a particular audience.

This point about accommodation versus authenticity was illustrated to me early in my career when I went to a presentation by a senior leader in my company. He said that there would be a time in our careers when we would walk into a meeting and must be willing to resign. He said there would be a time when someone would ask us to do something or see something that would be so counter to our values that we should be willing to resign our position rather than compromise. I have been lucky so far in my career that this did not happen. But I carry this thought into every meeting.

Being authentic is having the integrity to live your values, even at the risk of personal loss. Just knowing there is a possibility and being prepared to be willing to resign is a powerful focus for your integrity and authenticity.

So, how can you establish yourself as an authentic leader? I believe there are three factors: self-knowledge, self-disclosure, and seeking and acting on feedback. Self-knowledge includes being aware of your strengths, weaknesses, emotions, and feelings. It also includes knowledge of where you come from and knowing your values and principles that drive you. Self-knowledge gives you an understanding of who you are and where you come from, and it makes you comfortable in your own skin.

Some of the biggest problems I see with leaders is that they experience a disconnect between who they really are and who they pretend to be. This disconnect can cause them to experience a high degree of confusion and stress, as they spend most of their time outside their comfort zone. The emphasis here is that they spend most of their time in that uncomfortable state. It is important for growth to stretch yourself and step outside your comfort zone and learn new things. This is critical to enhancing your strengths and overcoming your weaknesses. Self-knowledge drives your self-confidence to help you stretch.

Some leaders experience the so-called "imposter syndrome." They feel they are not equipped to be there. They feel like an imposter or a fraud. They pretend to be something they are not, and the biggest fear is that they will be found out and people will expose them as a fraud.

As a leader, you may experience this imposter syndrome when you take a role of greater responsibility. You may start to doubt that you have the experience and qualifications to take on this bigger job. I think we all have this feeling at some point in our career. You may appear confident as viewed from the outside, but internally you feel self-doubt. This feeling is valuable to recognize, as it puts you into a good place to learn. It is a real problem if it persists and paralyzes you and your actions.

Having a solid understanding of yourself helps you recognize where the gaps are in what you need to learn or change to take on the new job. Start with the perspective of strength. What are your past experiences, your skills, your leadership ability, and values that form the basis of taking on the role or task? Do not forget that you may bring fresh insights to the role because of your lack of experience.

Next, what do you need to do to learn to be more effective in your new role? Being authentic comes from a genuine assessment of your strengths and areas for growth. You will feel like an imposter if you do not recognize your limitations and plan to fill the gaps. You are not authentic if you pretend to yourself or others that you know something when you do not. In my experience, leaders who say "I don't know" are sometimes more authentic than those who have all the answers all the time. As a leader, being overconfident is as dangerous as lack of confidence.

The second driver of authenticity is self-disclosure. Do not be afraid to show others your authentic self. There is value in leaders showing vulnerability and selectively showing their weaknesses. Self-disclosure also involves being yourself and demonstrating your strengths. Take care not to overuse your strengths or to get into the mindset that you have the only approach that will work. Listening to other people's ideas can enhance your strengths. There is a necessary balance here: Do not be afraid to disclose your strength, but not at the cost of being open to different ideas and approaches. After all, no one likes a know-it-all.

The third driver of authenticity is seeking and acting on feedback. Your authenticity is not something you judge yourself; it is others' perception of you. Seek feedback, listen carefully, and act on the feedback. Someone once said to me that feedback is a gift. If someone gives you feedback, it is an opportunity to learn and grow. Feedback is the only way to understand your positive presence. Being authentic involves knowing what others think of you and acting on their feedback.

Skills and Behaviors for Being Present in the Moment

Have you ever attended a meeting where half the people in the room look at their laptops? Or have you participated in a conference call where the background noise of someone typing gets everyone's attention because the individual forgot to put a device on mute? Perhaps you attended meetings where people constantly peek at their smartphones under the table. These are all clear signs that some people in the room are "not present." They do not pay full attention to the meeting or focus on the discussion. You suspect they focus on their social media feeds or emails.

You may ask yourself why you participate in a meeting that cannot engage people or waste your time on meetings that are not focused. On the other hand, you may ask yourself why participants attend meetings when they clearly would rather do something else. You may find that you are the one not paying full attention. I would argue that, under these conditions, half the meetings that you attend could end in half the time if everyone focuses, pays attention, and is "present."

What does it mean to be present? People write a lot of articles and books about being present, being mindful, paying attention. Mindfulness includes both secular and non-secular approaches and includes using yoga and meditation to focus the mind. These techniques are now in the mainstream of Western culture and professional life. I will share with you the value I took from studying these techniques and traditions as it applies to leadership. But, before looking at being present in the "now," let us think about the things that distract leaders from this goal.

ENERGIZE TO IMPACT

Distractions From Being Present in the Moment

You have thousands of thoughts each day. As with most people, most of these thoughts are of little value and distract you from being present in the moment. The first major distraction, or mindlessness, is getting lost in fantasy of the past or the future. Fantasy in the past involves second-guessing what happened in the past or regretting a decision or course of action you took. You do not have any control over what is in the past; the moment is gone. There is little value in spending a lot of time feeling guilt, having regrets, or rewinding the video of your past life. There is value in learning from the past and moving on.

Similarly, there is little value in worrying about the future and all the possible scenarios that may occur; you have little control over the future. It is of value, of course, to have a vision or a dream and know what you want to achieve and a plan to get there. But you can waste a lot of energy if you agonize over the future. Things will change in the future; the future will not be the same as the past or the present moment. If you focus on the present moment, you have a shot at maximizing the "now."

The most extreme example I experienced in my professional life related to mergers and acquisitions. I experienced three large mergers in the company where I worked. If you have yet to go through a merger or acquisition, the process goes something like this. First, there are rumors that that the company is in talks to merge with another company or be taken over. Often, the media first communicates this, and you may learn about it in a newspaper or online newsfeed. This can result in feelings of uncertainty about your job. People around you at work start to speculate about the future and, if you are not careful, this can be the only topic of conversation you hear.

The second phase is when the rumors become real and executives make announcements about the merger or acquisition. Your feelings of uncertainty become more real. Now you know it will happen, and you may start to speculate about future scenarios. These can range from fear of losing your job or being moved to a new location. You also start to question whether the new company will be involved in the type of work you do. People around you are fearful and start to try to understand the other company involved, including who works in what position at the other company. Naturally, you want to find out about people who may become competitors for your job. At this point, the rumors may continue for a year or more.

The third phase is when the potential merger goes through regulatory review, which often involves multiple countries around the world. The levels of uncertainty are still high. You may become obsessed with trying to predict the future in respect to your job, your organization, and your work. It is not uncommon for people around you to spend a lot of time speculating about the future, and they gossip around the water cooler. Under these conditions, creative thought and innovation could be paralyzed as your life feels like it is on hold.

In the final phase, the parties finalize the deal and form the new company. There is still a high level of uncertainty as you wait for decisions about what the new organization will look like. During this time, people will leave the organization voluntarily or be laid off. That situation adds to your stress of trying to keep your work moving forward.

In some cases, this uncertainty goes on for over two years. Throughout this process, it is difficult to focus on the "now" with so much uncertainty about the future over which you have little or no control. In some cases, people get trapped into staying through the process either to see if they have a good job in the new company or, if they have been with the company for many years, to hold out for a severance package.

Even under these extreme conditions, you gain nothing by fantasizing about the future and trying to predict outcomes. As a strategic leader, it is important to focus on what you can control. Helping your staff to focus on the present rather than speculate about future scenarios will help them to avoid the fear and agony that comes from long-term uncertainty. In business and in life, there will be times when there is pain. But there does not need to be suffering.

A second form of mindlessness is denying the inevitability that change and loss will happen. In the example of mergers and acquisitions, it is easy to think that nothing will change. You can expend a lot of energy thinking that it would be nice if nothing changed and things would stay the same. But change is inevitable.

Equally, change leads to loss of some kind (loss of job, loss of power, talent leaving, etc.) Again, loss is inevitable. Denying that loss and change will happen is a mindless activity. Enjoy the moment and plan for the future. Do not endlessly second-guess what may happen.

A good example of this inevitability is top performers on a team. I always say that we borrow great performers for a period. As a strategic leader, if you do your job well, you give them the opportunity to grow and develop. This inevitably means that they will move on to greater endeavors. Although this might be inconvenient or even painful for you, the opposite is worse and is a clear sign of a bad leader. If you try to hold back your top performers, you lose the opportunity of getting the most from them while they are with you, but you run the risk of their becoming frustrated and leaving anyway.

The third form of mindlessness I experienced is spending time and energy comparing yourself to others. "Keeping up with the Joneses" is a common way people become distracted from thinking about the present. They waste precious energy and capacity for thought. This often plays out in organizations with time spent on who has the biggest title or office. These status symbols may give you a certain level of satisfaction in the short term but seeking bigger and better status symbols can easily distract you from your purpose and mission. Some of the most heated discussions I experienced in organizational life were with people who were more interested in someone else's promotion or performance rating. Thinking about how they could grow and develop themselves rather than comparing themselves to others would be a better use of their time.

Another form of distraction from which we all suffer at times is impulsiveness. This occurs when the influences of other parts of your brain (including emotions) hijack your pre-frontal cortex and cloud your judgment. Being impulsive can have a negative impact on being present. If you make an impulsive decision or take impulsive action, you may regret the decision. You can start to be distracted by regret or guilt about your action and start to second-guess your decision. Spending energy thinking about past decisions can distract you from being present and in the moment. You should learn from the past and incorporate that learning into your future actions.

As a leader, one of the problems of being impulsive is that you may reflect on a decision and then change it. This can frustrate people working with you; and you may appear to be indecisive, unclear, and inconsistent in your actions. I am not against spontaneity and being flexible as situations change. But if a leader's dominant leadership style is impulsiveness, the leader ends up wasting a lot of time and energy. Being self-aware of your emotions and feelings will help you recognize when you are impulsive and what drives that impulsiveness.

Another type of distraction or mindlessness that gets in the way of being present in the moment is the tendency to take things personally. Your boss or colleague may make a comment or decision that you think aims at you personally. The comments we tend to take personally are ones we perceive as negative; we are less inclined to take positive comments as personal. We are naturally wired to have negativity biases.

The distraction comes in how you react to the comment. If you are present in the moment, you will address the comment, seeking understanding and clarity of the meaning, and address the issue there and then. If you perceive a negative comment that you take personally, you may withdraw and spend time and energy thinking about the comment. You may play the interaction over in your mind and may keep revisiting it, maybe wishing you reacted differently with a great reply or question. But if you take things personally, there is a danger of spending time reliving the past, regretting your reaction, and speculating what it means for the future. This wasted energy distracts you from being present.

In conclusion, there are many distractions that can be a barrier to focusing and being present in the moment. Fantasizing about the future and living in the past can be a distraction primarily because you have a low level of control. The future can bring multiple scenarios and uncertainty over which you have no control, and it can distract you from your present focus if you agonize or worry about what may happen. You can try to bring more control or reduce uncertainty by having a clear vision and plan, but your agility and resilience will come from taking each moment one at a time. Speculating about the future can waste valuable energy and, by not focusing on the present, you may not be prepared for the future.

Similarly, the past is gone, and you have no control over it. Regrets and guilt about your actions or decisions or about the situation you are in can distract you from making the most of the present. This does not mean that you do not learn from past moments to enhance your present moments. But you risk missing the present moments by being distracted by the past.

Other things that can distract you from making the most of the present and being mindful include denying the inevitability that change and loss will happen. We are hardwired to minimize loss and pursue pleasure. But a strategy in life to do this can lead to high levels of distress and suffering. Hedonism and loss avoidance can lead to getting lost in the pursuit and missing the richness of the present moment. Impulsiveness, taking things personally, and comparing yourself to others are also mindless thoughts that take you away from enjoying the present moment and distract you from today.

In my experience, focus and being present in the moment is not easy today and when working in complex organizations. I do not want to imply that being present in the moment is possible all the time. However, it is a goal that is worth pursuing. Many distractions result from our ability to communicate and obtain information at a faster rate than ever before because of the advances in technology. In a fast-moving, dynamic environment where nothing stands still and change seems constant, change often feels like chaos instead of progress. The challenge is to take advantage of communication and information technologies without being overwhelmed by the information.

We are invited to go down many "rabbit holes," and many of them are interesting and tempting. However, as a strategic leader, a key skill is identifying the urgent, critical information that needs to be top priority for your attention and is of the most value. In addition, you should be able to think critically about information, considering the source and supporting data. Being present in the moment is a skill that you can learn and develop.

Mindfulness and Being Present in the Moment

How can a leader be more mindful and be more present in the moment? Many people write about mindfulness and meditation techniques, and I suggest that you read further around these subjects. I argue that leaders should put aside some time in their busy day to focus their thinking using techniques like meditation. Focusing on being aware of the present moment by openly monitoring your thoughts is a good practice. In my experience, regular focus leads to the ability to control your thoughts and increase your attention. In fact, it is quite a breakthrough when you find yourself savoring a moment or seeing a detail in the world that you previously did not see.

The first advantage of being mindful is being open to experiences and staying open-minded. This comes from a heightened self-awareness. The second advantage is that feeling what is happening in the moment will inspire you to understand others' perspectives and identify other people's reactions and feelings. This, of course, is empathy, as discussed earlier. By seeing others' perspectives and feelings, it is possible to minimize a natural tendency to judge others.

A third advantage of being mindful is that you increase your level of self-control. Becoming aware of your feelings and reactions, and their triggers, enables you to monitor and control your behavior more effectively.

The fourth advantage of being self-aware and being mindful is that it helps you to accept a situation as it is. This is what some people refer to as "being with the itch," meaning you have the control to not scratch the itch. You can be present and be with whatever arises.

Another way of thinking about this comes from an acceptance of "it is what it is." There is a feeling of power sometimes when you can let go of what you cannot control. Conversely, you can expend a lot of energy on things you cannot control. Acceptance brings to mind the commonly quoted Serenity Prayer. ("God, grant me the serenity to accept the things I cannot change, courage to change things I can change, and wisdom to know the difference.")

Acceptance is an important concept in being mindful. As discussed earlier, a form of mindlessness is denying the inevitability of change and loss. Accepting what you can control, what the situation is, and that loss and change are inevitable is an important discipline in the ability of being present and focusing your attention.

The final advantage of being mindful is something we often forget to do in a fast-paced environment: treat yourself with loving-kindness. In other words, do not spend time beating yourself up for your perceived weaknesses. You can always learn to improve and take opportunities to grow.

Skills and Behaviors for Effective Listening

The ability to listen to other people is a critical skill for an energizing, impactful leaders, as it enables them to get the most out of their teams and people with whom they interact. A common expression is that "God gave us two ears and one mouth, so use them in that proportion." But true listening is more than that.

Listening is more than hearing sound or the words someone says. It means paying thoughtful attention to what someone says. Listening involves more than the ears; it also involves observation of body language and the subtle signs that add meaning to what someone communicates. It involves understanding the context of the message and the intent of the words. Listening also involves actively demonstrating that one is listening and understanding what someone says.

The incidents I mentioned earlier about people becoming distracted in meetings because of their smartphones is an example of someone who limits truly listening. They hear what a speaker says but focus more on the distraction. Because they do not listen actively, it is not uncommon for them to interrupt with unnecessary questions or comments. In my experience, this is common in leaders who are busy and do not want to hear other people's viewpoints. In contrast to such limited listening, leaders who actively listen can gain important information that can lead to resolving an issue or challenge.

Taking listening a step forward, energizing, impactful leaders apply their skill of empathizing. In my leadership coaching practice, I show how empathetic listening helps a leader gain a clear, accurate understanding of a situation, actions, and other people's thoughts and feelings. Remember, as a leader, you need this understanding before you can influence your followers to take the course of action necessary to achieve strategic goals. Paying attention to nonverbal reactions helps you understand their feelings.

Furthermore, empathetic listening helps you uncover and understand discrepancies in others' (and your own) core values and beliefs that initially may be unconscious beliefs. Empathetic listening helps you determine whether your audience understands you correctly.

What are the implications of these levels of listening on your ability to be an energizing, impactful leader? First, as discussed earlier, if you are not present in the moment and are preoccupied with other things, you significantly limit your ability to listen and get the full context and understanding of the message the speaker tries to communicate. If you jump in and interrupt when others speak, you will be destined to limit your ability to listen to the true meaning.

The same is true if your focus is thinking about the next thing you want to say rather than listening to others. If you have a preconceived idea of what you or another person will say, you close your thinking and risk missing an important point, a new idea, or a fresh perspective on a situation. You also close the opportunity to learn. In the most extreme cases, you will rely on stereotypes and personal prejudices to understand the world. In other words, you will demonstrate a closed mindset and limit your ability to have an open mindset.

Limited listening has an impact on your ability to lead others. If you are preoccupied or jump in when others talk, there is a risk that the speaker will feel you hear what the person says but that the person's ideas and views are not important to you. This can have an impact on employee engagement and your ability to influence others to follow your vision and strategic goals.

If you have a reputation for not listening, it has an impact on your ability to form productive relationships, and people may view you as not collaborative. A behavior that will cause others to perceive you as not listening is your giving the impression that the conversation is "all about me." Busy talking about yourself shows you do not value the other person's feelings or reactions.

The immature listening skills discussed above can have an impact on your ability to learn from others and have a de-motivating effect on those around you. In addition, dominating conversations and not listening to others can make you unapproachable. People may not want to interact with you and think that talking to you is a waste of time.

The danger here is that they may keep information you need. They may be aware of an issue but not bring it to your attention or tell you when an issue is beyond control until it may be too late to do anything about it. This would significantly limit your ability to proactively manage a problem and limit your options for a solution. It is much more difficult to manage surprises and unexpected circumstances. Therefore, not listening is a significant risk to you as a strategic leader and may have a negative impact on your ability to deliver your goals.

The second point to consider as a leader is that listening must be intentional. Listening is a skill that leaders can develop. Some people are more natural and intuitive when it comes to recognizing subtle signs and reactions in others, but this is a skill any leader can work on improving. The journey to effective leadership starts with a commitment to want to be better at listening. This commitment must come from a genuine interest in hearing what others say and noticing how they act. Listening genuinely and intensely to someone else is part of being authentic as a leader.

Just like being present in the moment, leaders need to put aside time to genuinely listen. This is not always possible in a busy schedule but should be an aspiration. In my coaching practice, I make a commitment to people I coach that I will be present for them during our sessions. I work to make this a reality by not scheduling another meeting or reading email for fifteen minutes ahead of our session. This allows me to clear my mind of distractions and focus on the upcoming discussions.

I also request that people I coach do the same and not run from a meeting into our session. The reality is that this is not always possible. But my clients and I agree that if something distracts them or me, such as needing to put out a fire at work (not literally we hope), then I would rather reschedule the session, even at the last minute. In my experience, this practice leads to a more intense and productive session.

The third point to consider about effective listening as a leader is that it is easier to achieve in a face-to-face encounter. The conditions of how you meet can have an impact on your ability to listen effectively. Obviously, it is difficult to listen if you are in a noisy or crowded area. To optimize your ability to listen, you should meet in a private area for the discussion, which would make you and the other person comfortable. Sit opposite each other, facing toward each other at a slight angle. This allows you to observe body language. It is also helpful to avoid having a table between you. Sitting on opposite sides of a table can cause a feeling that there is a barrier between the two of you. If you meet with a larger team, choose a place that has good acoustics and where everyone is visible to each other.

Obviously, in most interactions, particularly with individuals who are not in the same geographical locations, face-to-face discussions are not always possible. My experience is that a face-to-face meeting for an individual or a new team, if possible, should occur at the start of a relationship. The leader allow time to get to know the others. In that meeting, it is possible to pick up some pointers on how the other person or team members react and behave.

Following that meeting, if continuing face-to-face meetings is not possible, it is useful to meet by video conference. Modern video-conferencing cameras are sensitive, and it is possible to listen at higher levels with practice and experience. Telephone communication is more difficult for picking up subtle reactions.

Whether you listen in face-to-face meetings, by video conference, or by telephone, it is critical that you get feedback to ensure that you succeeded in communicating the right message. To trigger feedback, ask questions, summarize what was said, and check for clarity of meaning.

Independent of the mode of communication, leaders must develop and refine the skills needed to listen effectively. Energizing, impactful leaders intentionally seek to listen effectively. It is good practice to be conscious of your level of listening in any given situation and to practice the skills required to facilitate your listening skills. As with several skills and behaviors identified in this book, it is a good idea to keep a journal and reflect on what goes well in each interaction and what you can do differently.

Skills and Behaviors for Influencing Others and for Power Dynamics

Energizing, impactful leaders with positive presence intentionally act, communicate, listen, and manage their visibility. Through positive presence, effective leaders build and manage trust in their relationships with their team, peers, senior leaders, and collaborators, both inside and outside their organization. Their authenticity and being present in the moment helps them build trust and credibility.

As a leader, your positive presence is valuable because it influences others to follow you to achieve your purpose, your vision, and your strategic goals. Influence is a form of power that one person tries to exercise over others to try to persuade them to follow a course or to do things that they may not immediately want to do. Influence provides motivation and direction. Leaders who use authoritative power try to do the same thing, but there is a big difference between influence and authoritative power.

Using authoritative power comes from being in a position of power due to a hierarchy or reporting relationship. Most of the time, authoritarian behaviors are disrespectful of others. These leaders have a feeling of superiority. They provide direction through orders. They frequently criticize employee performance. They do not listen to employees' viewpoints. Their motivating actions often rely on punishments for people who do not follow the leader's orders. Authoritarian leadership behavior quickly causes employee unhappiness, low morale, dissatisfaction with the job, and employees exiting the company.

In contrast to authoritarian behaviors, influencing behaviors of energizing, impactful leaders create a positive environment that encourages employees to want to follow the leader's direction. These leaders respect others and often take a collaborative approach to achieving strategic goals. They motivate employees through a compelling vision and frequent measurements of progress in achieving goals. They do not just talk; they listen effectively. Their behavior demonstrates that they will support the team on the journey to achieve strategic goals.

Influence is especially necessary for accomplishing goals in today's business world because organizations now depend on cross-functional teams, third-party service providers, joint ventures, and collaborative partners. Each entity has separate authorities. In today's business world, your ability to influence and persuade others in such blended operational environments is a crucial skill.

Before we explore the subject of influence further, I want to remind you that effective leaders behave with authenticity. Being authentic must be a foundation in the way you influence your followers. As I pointed out earlier, part of being authentic means you do not manipulate others into following you, either by using tricks or authoritative behaviors. You must avoid being disingenuous when trying to influence others. Not demonstrating authenticity in your efforts to persuade your followers to follow your strategic goal and plans will negatively impact your reputation and compromise your trustworthiness.

Influencing others necessitates that you first feel personally powerful. Why? Because people who feel powerful have a positive presence. I already described the importance of a positive presence.

Think of examples of some people you believe are powerful. What characteristics do they usually display? They are self-confident. They talk optimistically and talk about winning. They do not make excuses when presenting their expectations. They appear composed rather than overwhelmed or stressed in a crisis. They appear focused and not distracted by changing circumstances around them. And, obviously, they are highly successful. How does this feeling, and display of personal power happen? Is it a mostly a matter of personality traits?

A key factor in developing a feeling of personal power is simply adopting that feeling. What enables you to adopt it? Certain aspects, such as this book advocates, are necessary for effective leadership such as a high degree of self-awareness, continual mindfulness (especially of what is happening in the moment) and being intentional about listening. Seeking feedback and acting on it also helps build your feeling of power. Feedback can cue you into important decision-making factors, and it helps you understand the power of your communications.

Feeling personally powerful is essential for feeling and displaying confidence in the mission, purpose, and strategic goals in which you believe and essential in inspiring others to follow you. Feeling personally powerful is the first step to influencing others.

CHARLES S. DORMER

Energizing, Impactful Leadership in Action: Ensuring Positive Presence

It was almost an after-thought when Megan walked into a lecture theatre five years ago on a Friday afternoon to listen to a visiting professor's lecture on her latest research. Megan was in her second year as a post-doctoral student at the university she attended for her PhD, researching practical applications of cutting-edge science in medical devices. She enjoyed the mixture of pure science and engineering that resulted from her studies. She was not totally clear as to what she wanted to do. She knew she wanted to impact the world but was not clear about how she could do that.

Waiting for the lecture to begin, she aimlessly checked her email and social media feeds. Her smartphone still had her attention when the lecture began. But she quickly realized this was not a normal lecture, a dry retelling of an obscure piece of research. The professor presented her latest research resulting from working with other departments at her university.

Her research resulted in forming several small companies to develop and commercialize the science from her laboratory and other broad-based laboratories in her area. The professor explained that the creation of intellectual property and commercialization of her research was an important part of her role as a teacher and researcher. This was the way she would use her research to help people with untreatable illnesses that impacted their quality of life.

It was not just the content of the lecture that left an impression on Megan. The professor's positive presence in the room also inspired Megan. Her passion and enthusiasm for her work was clear from her presentation. Her self-confidence and natural, gentle, relaxed style inspired Megan. Megan was intrigued about the science but also recognized that she could learn a lot from the professor as a scientist and as a leader.

After the lecture, Megan took the opportunity to meet the professor and ask some questions about her research and her methods of collaboration with other laboratories. They exchanged business cards, and the professor agreed to meet Megan to discuss her career. This was the start of a mentoring relationship that lasted five years.

During the next year or so, they met for lunch and discussed opportunities in the professor's laboratory once Megan finished her degree. Megan knew the professor's standards for her staff were high. Her staff needed stellar resumes but also had to demonstrate that they could collaborate with others. Megan worked hard to collaborate in her current role. Eventually, she accepted a position working for the professor.

Megan's first impression of her new mentor was her presence when she entered a room. Her ability to collaborate with many people also impressed Megan. She knew that she could learn a great deal not only from a science perspective but also about leadership.

From the beginning, Megan viewed the professor as being a "nice" person. She was authentic and always had time to listen to everyone. She made others feel comfortable in interactions with her and yet challenged them to think outside the box. She had a clear vision of what she wanted to achieve and motivation to achieve her goals. She was always optimistic and did not let setbacks distract her.

Megan could not remember a time when she saw her mentor stressed in any situation. The professor always gave the impression that she knew how her behavior impacted others. She had a high degree of self-awareness and carefully and thoughtfully managed her behavior.

From Megan's perspective, her mentor's most impressive characteristic was that she was always present, whether she was talking to a big group in a large meeting or in a one-on-one conversation. She did not read her email or look around the room for other people to talk to; she was present and focused on talking to the person or group in the meeting.

The professor was in the moment, focused on what was in front of her at that time. In fact, when she talked about a problem or issue, she spoke in the present tense. She wanted to learn from past experiences and see a vision for the future, but she focused on the "now" situation. She did not spend time regretting past decisions or speculate about things that could go wrong in the future. She focused on now. She also had the ability to listen intensely to what others had to say. She did not immediately jump in with her idea or solution before listening to all viewpoints and perspectives.

Megan's interactions with her mentor were intense and focused, but not in a way that made her feel threatened. Although the professor looked Megan directly in the eye with a steely intensity, there was also a warmth that made Megan feel special. The professor had the ability to make Megan feel that she was totally present for Megan in that moment. She appeared open and honest with Megan, expressing her true feelings and thoughts. She was always open to ideas, no matter the source. If Megan had an idea, her mentor listened intensely to her thoughts.

Megan also admired her mentor's ability to build relationships and network with a wide range of people, both inside and outside the university and the professor's area of expertise. She was not threatened by not being the expert in the room.

The professor also built trust quickly, which resulted in some highly successful collaborations. She always talked about the "big picture," did not get involved in the details, and was not a micro-manager.

Finally, Megan appreciated that her mentor was very generous with her time, ideas, information, knowledge, and gave credit where it was due. She also shared the rewards of success and shared equity in her start-up companies with her collaborators and staff.

Megan trusted her mentor and wanted to follow her vision. She trusted her with career choices and where to focus her energy. Megan was a smart, young women and had choices for where she should work and where she would put her attention and energy.

A key reason Megan chose to work with the professor was her leadership skills. A key quality Megan admired was the professor's authenticity. It helped to build trust and motivated Megan to keep following the professor. Her authentic style of being confident, transparent, open, and honest, generous, and being open to feedback and ideas from others had an impact on recruiting and retaining her best talented people. It also had an impact on her team's productivity. Megan was energized and passionate about the work. She felt challenged, yet comfortable taking a risk and thinking outside the box. Being an authentic leader was an important element to building an innovative, engaged, and motivated workforce.

Megan perceived that the professor's positive presence "in the room" inspired her and others to follow the professor. Her self-confidence, knowledge of science, charisma, authenticity, passion, and enthusiasm made everyone with whom she interacted feel that they were special. Her behaviors demonstrated her gravitas, or seriousness, which made her followers realize they should regard what she said as important. Simply put, the professor demonstrated that she had a level of power, and it enabled her to create energy in others.

Her gravitas partly came from her credibility, which came from her technical competence and her knowledge of science, the papers she wrote, and other demonstrations of her expertise. Megan recognized that credibility is more than just knowledge and that it relies on authenticity, believability, and trust demonstrated in interactions. Megan also recognized the professor's self-confidence and decisiveness. She always seemed calm, competent, and in control, even when she was in a stressful situation. The professor also possessed charisma—personal magnetism, and charm—which enabled her to inspire enthusiasm and passion with people with whom she interacted.

Megan found a real role model with her professor, and she learned a lot from her about being a great leader. As Megan progressed in her leadership journey, she felt that she knew what success looked like. Megan reflected on her own leadership gaps and, with the help of a coach, she worked on her development plan to build her positive presence like her professor.

Chapter Summary

Effective leaders are aware of the impact of their behavior. They maximize positive impacts and minimize negative impacts.

Positive presence is the way you intentionally act, communicate, listen, and manage in interactions. It is how you show up to build and manage trust. The impact of your positive presence is to ethically influence others (whether under your direct control or not) to buy into and deliver on your purpose and strategic goals. A positive-presence model consists of content and communication, visibility, and behaviors that result in trust and influence. Trust comes from being your authentic self, being present in the moment, and intentional listening.

Positive presence involves having credibility through self-confidence, knowledge, gravitas, passion, and enthusiasm, and remaining calm under stress. It also involves a style of communication that is clear and intentional and presents a compelling story or narrative to the audience. Leaders with a positive presence also use humor appropriately to add energy to the communication.

A positive presence also involves nonverbal as well as verbal communications, and this includes body language, posture, and dress. A key outcome of your communications, actions, and having a positive presence is building and managing trust in relationships. Trust is the most valuable asset in your reputation, and you must build your reputation. You need to protect and cherish a good reputation and trustworthiness.

You build trust by being authentic. It involves understanding your authentic self and acting in a way that is consistent with your values. Other people judge your authenticity, so you must be aware of what others think and feel about you. It requires a high degree of self-awareness to really understand your strengths, weaknesses, thoughts, emotions, and where you come from. Another aspect of authenticity is being courageous enough to feel comfortable disclosing your true self and showing vulnerability.

A positive presence also requires that you be present in the moment. You must focus on the moment and not become distracted by agonizing about the past or worrying about the future. You should learn from past experiences and plan for the future, but you must recognize that change is inevitable, and loss occurs in change.

Being present in the moment also means you do not allow yourself to become distracted by comparing yourself to others or taking things personally.

A positive presence involves intentionally listening and developing active and empathetic listening. You must manage others' contributions to discussions (verbal and written communication) and value quality over quantity. By listening effectively, you show that you are open to input and ideas from others and can learn from diverse sources.

The most important outcome of a positive presence is the ability to influence others to be part of a purpose and deliver on strategic goals. This involves understanding and feeling your personal power and using it appropriately. The difference between influencing power and authoritative power is that you are open-minded and influenced by good ideas from other people, independent of the source of the idea.

Understanding the impact of your behavior and ensuring you have a positive presence is a skill you learn and develop. It takes self-reflection and feedback to fully appreciate how you can do this effectively.

Key Learnings About Having a Positive Presence

- Energizing, impactful leaders influence others to follow their purpose and strategic goals by being aware and managing their positive presence.
- They are aware of the impact of their behavior on others. They intentionally act, communicate, and listen in ways that show a positive impact on others.
- They build and manage trust in their relationships.
- They are authentic (attuned to their most sincere selves even under stress).
- They are present in the moment.

Action Plan for Having a Positive Presence

In your action plan, take time to reflect on your strengths and your opportunity for growth. This self-reflection has two parts. First, review the following questions and rate yourself for a strength or an opportunity for growth for each question. Next, think about actions that you can take to enhance your strength or develop your opportunity for growth.

1. Are you calm and competent, even under stress?
2. Do you inspire enthusiasm and passion in others?
3. Do you proactively and intentionally try to understand your audience?
4. Do you present your case as a story or narrative?
5. Do you intentionally strive to create and manage trust with others by sharing information, recognizing excellence, and delegating without micromanaging?
6. Do you work to be perceived as authentic (show your authentic self)?
7. Do you spend excessive time agonizing about the past or worrying about the future?
8. Do you recognize the inevitability that things will change, and loss will happen?
9. Do you intentionally work to listen effectively?
10. Do you use power appropriately (influencing ethically and not making others powerless)?
11. Do you communicate intentionally so that your nonverbal and verbal messages are consistent?

Chapter 6
Creating a Positive Environment

"Health is the first of all liberties, and happiness gives us the energy which is the basis of health."

Henri Amiel, Swiss philosopher, and writer
("Journal intime," April 3, 1865)

Effective leaders seek ways to maximize the impact of their strategies. One way is to create a positive environment that encourages people to thrive and develop their talent to their full potential. They create circumstances and conditions that generate positive energy, whether their group is local or global.

Prior chapters discussed the need to understand yourself and develop an inner reflection on your strengths, weaknesses, mindset, feelings, and emotional triggers. Prior chapters also focused on the impact of your behavior and how you manage your visibility to develop a positive presence, which leads to enhanced levels of trust, authenticity, communication, listening, and being present in the moment.

Now we move on to consider a third important aspect of leadership: the need to create positive energy by establishing an environment that encourages others to thrive and develop, an environment where others want to be part of delivering your purpose and strategic goals.

I worked with a university student intern in conducting a small research project looking at leadership in the pharmaceutical industry. When we asked survey respondents about critical factors for leadership, one commented that leaders should create a positive environment that fosters inclusion and open dialogue. The respondent suggested that leaders who develop this characteristic bring more to the table and that underusing inclusion and open dialogue impacts an organization's productivity.

From my personal experience, I agree that it is more productive to work in an environment that encourages employees to be creative and empowers them to do meaningful and important work. The opposite situation can be stifling and disengaging. A key leadership skill is the ability to create a positive environment that encourages innovation and creativity to deliver strategic purpose and goals.

Characteristics of a Positive Environment

So, what does a positive environment look like? Let us consider this question from three angles: outcome, positive energy, and environment.

First, from an outcome perspective, a positive environment is one where you get the most out of the people in your organization. It is one where you take advantage of the talents and ideas of the people with whom you work (either internal or external to your organization). It is an environment where everyone is engaged and motivated to deliver on the organization's purpose and strategic goals. It is an environment where everyone can thrive and develop. It is an environment that encourages innovation and creativity but also focuses on delivering on a strategic purpose and strategic goals. It has a level of management control that does not stifle innovation.

Second, positive environment relates to creating positive energy. Energizing, impactful leaders understand how energy works in their organization. They know how to create positive energy and minimize the impact of events or distractions that create negative energy. You can create positive energy by having an inspirational purpose and strategic goals (as discussed in the chapters about strategic and system thinking). Your behavior as a leader also influences energy creation (as discussed in the chapter about positive presence). Leaders who are aware of their positive presence and have a high degree of self-awareness can have an impact on the energy of the people with whom they interact.

ENERGIZE TO IMPACT

In the past, I adopted the practice of walking through the laboratory I supervised and getting a feel for the energy of the group. This proved to be useful, as it gave me an opportunity to touch base with my employees in a social way. It also gave me the opportunity to directly address issues that could cause negative energy in the group. It is worth touching base with your group regularly and starting the interaction by getting the feel for the energy level of the group.

The final point to consider when defining positive environment is the meaning of the word "environment." Merriam-Webster.com defines environment as "the aggregate of social and cultural conditions that influence the life of an individual or community." The environment I describe in this book has all the conditions that surround a work environment. These include all interactions within the system, whether it is face to face, virtual meetings, written communications including emails, and group and individual interactions. It also includes the physical and virtual spaces involved in the work environment.

Creating a positive environment involves a leader creating circumstances and conditions that encourage innovation and creativity. A positive environment will lead to a positive culture for the long term. Aspects of the environment that are under a leader's control include how the leader's behavior impacts the environment. Some aspects that will negatively impact the organization are outside the leader's control. The role of a strategic leader in this case is to minimize the negative energy.

For example, there may be major change going on such as restructuring or mergers and acquisitions that are outside a leader's control and could have a negative impact on the organization. The role of the leader in this case is to minimize the impact of the changes and keep individuals in the organization focused on what they can control. As I mentioned previously, pain occurs in most organizations, but that does not mean there must be suffering.

Three Factors that Impact Creation of a Positive Environment

To recap: In a positive environment, a leader creates positive energy for conditions and circumstances that are under the leader's control and minimizes negative energy for those that are not. The leader makes the most of diversity of experiences and ideas through the inclusion of everyone and facilitates individuals becoming as productive as possible. The result of a positive environment is that individuals are engaged and motivated, they thrive and develop their talents, and they deliver on their strategic purpose and strategic goals.

With this definition of positive environment in mind, let us now explore three factors that impact the creation of a positive environment. First, create an environment where everyone can thrive. Second, be inclusive and access diversity in ideas, backgrounds, and experience. Third, be intentional in creating positive physical and virtual environments.

Factor 1: Create an Environment Where Everyone Can Thrive

One of the factors that leaders often overlook is the need to create an environment where everyone can thrive. Just like you as an energizing, impactful leader, others work more productively if they are not distracted and can focus on the work at hand. As a leader, you should avoid being a distraction to your employees. You can help with focus by setting clear goals that are appropriately challenging for your team. It is my experience that if goals are too easy, there is not a lot of satisfaction or sense of achievement. On the other hand, setting goals that are too difficult or perceived as impossible will have a demotivating effect.

As a leader, you also can reduce levels of uncertainty, particularly during times of great change, by being open and honest about what is known and what is not known. As discussed in a previous chapter, greater focus comes from being present in the moment. In addition, you can protect your team from unnecessary and distracting organizational politics. Leaders should reduce the "drama" that is prevalent in organizations.

As discussed earlier, it is important that a leader have a high degree of self-confidence and an open mindset. The same applies for other people in their teams.

In creating an environment where people can thrive, you as the leader should build self-confidence in others. You should not give the impression that you judge others. If people feel judged, they are less likely to be creative and try new things.

It is valuable to give feedback close to the time of the action. I worked with leaders who can effectively give feedback to their co-workers, but they give the feedback long after an event. Only giving feedback as part of an annual performance review is an example of how not to motivate employees. This is less effective in creating a positive environment.

As I mentioned earlier, an effective leader must have a high degree of self-confidence that helps eliminate anxieties around failure. Similarly, an effective leader reduces the team's worries about failure. As the leader, you need to explain to employees that failure provides an opportunity to learn how to do things differently.

If the team worries about failure, performance reviews, and job consequences, they will do what is safe and not what is creative. An atmosphere of "failure is not an option" paralyzes creativity and hinders the flow to the desired impact. (By the way, this is particularly true in mergers and acquisitions or major reorganizations where individuals must re-apply for their jobs and are judged by a new group of people.)

Speaking of organizational change, leaders need to keep in mind that employees experience a high degree of uncertainty around job security and stability. This hinders their ability to be creative and feel fulfilled in their work. In an earlier chapter, I discussed the significant impacts of downsizing experiences including "survivor guilt" and disrupting established social networks.

Factor 2: Ensure Diversity and Inclusion

The second factor to consider as an energizing, impactful leader when creating a positive environment is how to ensure access to a diverse range of experiences, backgrounds, and ideas, and create an environment where everyone feels included. A lot of written material exists about the value of diversity in organizations, and this book does not review this literature.

There are numerous studies that present evidence of the need for, and benefits of, diversity and inclusion in an organization. For example, it can result in ideas for innovative new products or services that create more revenue and new ways to enter the market. It can result in improving customer satisfaction. Companies now recognize more than ever before that if they want to bring creative solutions to complex problems, they need a broad range of ideas that come from many sources and different ways of thinking. As Albert Einstein advised, "We cannot solve our problems with the same level of thinking that created them."

Organizations that lack diversity end up trying to solve problems with a narrow scope of thinking that restricts understanding of the problems and limits potential solutions. In contrast, organizations that ensure diversity benefit from everyone bringing an individual way of thinking about a problem, a way of framing a problem, and a limited set of biases to potential solutions. Diverse backgrounds and experiences open the possibility of thinking about a problem in a different way and using a different lens to think about a solution.

A good example of this benefit is the business of drug discovery. Developing a new drug involves understanding the science of disease, finding an active agent that will impact the disease, and testing for safety and efficacy in the patient populations that will benefit from use of the therapy. If the aim is to discover and develop a drug for patients throughout the world, then it is important have a global understanding of the disease and its treatment. Depending on local medical practices, doctors may diagnose and treat a disease in a different way. Access to medicine is quite different in a poor village in India versus in a large Western city.

Having access to people with diverse understanding, experiences, and backgrounds will bring different perspectives to developing a drug for worldwide use. There is no point to having a drug to treat influenza that must be used within 24 hours of first symptoms if patients must wait a week to see a prescribing doctor. Equally, there is little value in developing a drug that must be refrigerated if the disease is prevalent in areas where refrigerators are not common. The point: Everyone brings a certain set of strengths; but organizations must supplement those strengths with a diverse set of ideas, backgrounds, and experiences if they want to find innovative and creative solutions.

Energizing, impactful leaders recognize that diversity and inclusion impacts productivity in a positive way. Diverse thinking, experiences, and backgrounds that people in your team or collaborative relationships bring to the table ensures you as the leader can leverage different perspectives, ideas, and solutions to complex problems.

It should be noted that there is little value to diversity if you as the leader fail to take full advantage of the different views and perspectives that people bring to the table. There is also a significant negative impact if you exclude certain talent. Excluding certain individuals not only hurts their self-esteem but also reduces your effectiveness in developing talent in your organization. As an energizing, impactful leader, you need to create a positive environment that includes all viewpoints.

Diversity and inclusion work best when teams and organizations are multi-cultural and include people from different genders, ages, races, and religions. I emphasize the point that teams should be multicultural. But there is a danger if the team spends too much time talking about differences, as factions may form. As a leader creating a positive environment, you must make every effort to give everyone the opportunity to join in discussions among the common group.

As explained earlier, part of ensuring you have a positive presence is having a leadership style that is open to new ideas, independent of the source of the idea, and valuing everyone's input. Leadership skills are critical to ensuring inclusion in a diverse organization. It is also important to give positive feedback and recognition that lifts people up and makes them feel valued. As discussed in an earlier chapter, there are dangers if you do not ensure an inclusive environment. When employees have the impression that there is an in-group in which they are not included, it makes them feel powerless.

Factor 3: Intentionally Create Differences in Physical and Virtual Workspaces

The third factor to consider when creating a positive environment depends on whether the workspace is physical or virtual. Physical spaces include offices, cubicles, or open-space offices used by all levels of staff. If a primary enabler of your work is collaboration, open-space offices encourage people to talk to each other and can be highly effective. However, this style of office space can be too noisy and can distract people who are trying to read or write. If these spaces become quiet, they rather defeat the purpose of the collaboration aim of the space.

Quiet spaces must be available for people whose work requires focus on writing or reading. Offices should provide space for confidential discussions. Conference rooms are valuable for closed meeting or telephone conferences. Make sure you design the space for the nature of the work. A positive environment encourages creativity, innovation, and collaboration.

In my experience, most interactions today involve working with people who are not in the same room. This includes groups that access talent from many locations across the globe or work with individuals who may work at a remote office or at home. There are, of course, many advantages to working virtually. It gives us the opportunity to work with people at distant locations that could not occur in the past. By working with people in many different parts of the world, we can create a truly diverse workforce.

Being able to create a positive environment in a virtual sense is a key skill for leaders today. The COVID-19 pandemic crisis, which shifted many employees to work from home, demonstrated the effectiveness of many innovative new electronic communication tools However, a significant challenge of working virtually is the feeling of isolation. When employees work remotely and do not have day-to-day interactions with other people in the group, they can feel "out of the loop" on several issues.

How can you set up a positive environment in the virtual space? You and your teams must work together and collaborate to achieve your strategic goals, even if they are in a different office, different building, at home, or even on a different continent. Furthermore, how can you ensure a high level of productivity in a virtual environment?

Be Intentional in Leading in a Virtual Environment

In my experience, leaders who are successful in the virtual space have a plan of how to make the most of the technology but are aware that people, not technology, make the difference. These leaders are intentional in their actions and behaviors about managing virtual collaborations and do not assume that virtual teams will work without putting effort into making them work. They accept the challenge of this kind of environment. Many of these points also apply to working in the same physical location.

One challenge is that leaders must also be good managers, but traditional management models based on hierarchy and organizations that are top-down driven do not succeed in this kind of environment. For example, information flow cannot go up through a leader and filter down to the rest of the group. Subtle connections and information flow need to happen within the group at all levels, which can cause leaders to feel they do not know everything. Virtual teams are more like matrices of connectivity rather than the traditional pyramid. Technology creates new management models that facilitate information flow up, down, and across an organizational structure.

Communicating in a Virtual Environment

The critical leadership role of creating a positive virtual environment that ensures diversity and inclusion necessitates defining a common purpose, finding common ground, and defining clear goals. In a virtual environment, you as the leader must identify common ground that binds the group. You also must behave in a way that demonstrates you listen to all views and are open to all viewpoints.

Technology communication tools enable effective virtual communications. However, you should not assume everyone has the necessary level of competence with the technology. For example, millennials may have a higher level of skills and more experience using technology than baby boomers. You need to bring everyone up to a minimum level of skills. Building skills in this area is a priority, and you need to ensure everyone builds time into their schedule for training and gaining experience.

You also should be aware that people react to virtual technology in different ways. For example, people who are introverted may be uncomfortable on camera. They may become distracted by being on camera or may become even more reserved. It is important to be aware of these dynamics and put effort into making everyone feel included and comfortable in the opportunity to contribute.

The bottom line for all the points made above is that even with great technology success is still about people. Therefore, for large projects or projects that will continue for a significant length of time, it is valuable to have an in-person meeting (if possible) at least at the start of a virtual group working together.

Avoiding Exclusion in a Virtual Environment

As I mentioned earlier, leaders working with a virtual group must be even more intentionally inclusive. When people are not collocated, there is a risk that some will feel isolated or that their voice will not be heard.

An example I experienced is what I refer to as "head office syndrome." This occurs when part of the virtual group sits in the head office where the leader sits most of the time. Employees in that location have the advantage (most of the time) of physically seeing the leader more often. They encounter the leader getting coffee or at other times. It is easy for the leader and those co-located with the leader to informally chat about issues in the absence of others who are not located at the "head office."

I strongly recommend that you resist making decisions with a local group and informing the rest of the team afterwards. If this happens on a regular basis, it is easy for your group to perceive that there is an "in-group" and an "out-group." This may lead to the out-group feeling isolated and excluded.

For effective leadership in a virtual environment, you need to monitor the participation of everyone in the virtual group. Be intentionally inclusive and make sure you include everyone in the discussion. When people do not get a chance to talk, invite them to contribute. Do not let a few individuals dominate meetings or other media. Do not let a larger group dominate the few who are not at a single location.

To avoid people feeling excluded, as the leader, you also must be conscious of time differences and need to understand local cultures. If you have a global team, be aware that you may expect colleagues to join early in the morning or late at night (European or North American meeting with Asian participants). If you are on the East Coast of the United States and call a meeting at 8:00 a.m., do not expect your West Coast colleagues to be totally awake or alert.

Managing Conversation Rhythm In a Virtual Environment

The lack of communication cues based on body language is also a factor you must consider in respect to being inclusive in a virtual setting. During an in-person interaction, most people pick up on body language cues and see the reaction to communications. There is rhythm to a back-and-forth discussion among two or more people, which conveys not only what they say but also the tone of the communication and the physical reactions of the participants. This rhythm is more difficult to judge in virtual communications, with email being the most difficult and video conferencing being slightly easier. If the behaviors in virtual communications are not monitored, it affects the rhythm and can lead to people interrupting or speaking over each other or some people being silent. It is this second point that can have the biggest impact on inclusion.

If someone does not participate in the discussion, you may miss out on some great ideas or perspectives that remain unsaid. As a leader of a virtual group, you should be aware of the rhythm of the conversation and pull everyone into the conversation. Bear in mind that not everyone thinks in the same way, so you should build in time for people to reflect on what others say. Some people will need to think through a point before they contribute.

Be open and inclusive in the way you communicate and keep checking in with all the participants. In a virtual setting, it is especially important to make sure communication is clear, direct, and open. Focus the group on clear communication and check with others for understanding of both content and intent of messages. I see many leaders make the mistake in virtual settings of assuming that when people do not say anything, they agree with what is said. Do not assume silence is agreement.

As you monitor the rhythm of communications, be aware of when the conversation diverges or converges. Divergence is when the ideas flow and the discussion opens to input from everyone. Convergence is when the discussion focuses on reaching a decision or conclusion.

A conversation can start with getting everyone's opinion and input to the subject of the conversation (divergence). Once that happens, the open conversation may close to focus on getting to an outcome. This sequence of divergence-convergence can happen multiple times during a meeting. If, after everyone thinks divergence is finished and the group converges on a conclusion, it can derail the dynamics if someone throws in an additional comment to open divergence again. This may be a sign that someone lacked an opportunity to give input or needed time to process and reflect on the information discussed.

As the leader of a virtual group, you can manage these dynamics by setting a time limit on divergence. You might say, for instance, "We will open this up for discussion for thirty minutes, at which time we will close down for a decision." Also, you can make the group aware of which stage they are in at any given time.

During the divergence phase, it is important to be inclusive and ask for everyone's input. This dynamic exists when in a meeting or when opening a discussion by email or in a virtual team discussion database. As the leader, you have the same role in either case: be aware of the dynamics and move the group from divergent to convergent thinking at the appropriate time.

Managing Group Size in a Virtual Environment

Another point to consider around being inclusive in a virtual sense is that you need to create an environment where everyone can take part. If the group is too large to get everyone's input, you should consider having breakout discussions or forming sub-teams. In a break-out discussion, you split the group into several smaller groups to discuss an issue. You can then present the conclusions from the break-out sessions to the whole group. This strategy is effective when you want input on several issues and have divergent thinking.

Video technology tools are useful in launching break-out sessions from the main video meeting. As the leader, you have the opportunity to select who is in each of the groups, based on the issue to be discussed and the experience and personality of the participants. Remember to ask the groups to select someone to give feedback back to whole group; otherwise, there may an embarrassing silence until someone steps up to present.

Setting Group Ground Rules in a Virtual Environment

In addition to the leadership behaviors that facilitate creating a positive virtual environment, the virtual group members can help facilitate effectiveness. Group members should agree to ground rules on how they will work virtually. The rules are a set of agreed principles that the team will follow.

A good example of a ground rule is that everyone should agree to be present in the moment when the group meets virtually. In a phone call, for instance, a clear sign that someone is not present is the sound of clicking on a keyboard because someone forgets to mute the phone. It may not be true always, but people often use the opportunity in a virtual meeting to catch up with their email. In my experience, meeting times can be shortened, and productivity increased considerably if everyone is present in the moment and focuses on the work at hand rather than being distracted. A good ground rule for the group is that people turn off their phones and do not read emails during the meeting.

ENERGIZE TO IMPACT

Energizing, Impactful Leadership Action Plan: Creating a Positive Environment

Mo was the head of a mid-sized IT company. In his first year in this role, he worked hard and was pleased with the progress of his team and their research. He reflected on the times in his career when he worked in an environment that encouraged creativity and innovation. He remembered working for Joe, his first boss during his post-doctoral studies

Working in Joe's lab was one of the happiest and most productive times of Mo's life. Joe created a positive environment for his team and partners, one that allowed them to thrive and be creative. Joe took two actions to minimize the impact of uncertainty and change from major upheavals happening in the organization at that time because of a shift in the research climate.

First, Joe made sure he reacted to changes in the business environment in a measured and controlled way. He adjusted and ensured flexibility to changing needs and kept a high level of stability in the system. Second, Joe protected everyone from being impacted by the day-to-day organizational politics and power struggles that led to uncertainty about the future of the organizational structure or team and changing work priorities.

Joe created an environment that encouraged individuals to be positive by setting clear goals, providing real-time feedback, and balancing challenges and skill development. He also minimized disruptions, protected his employees, and reframed failure as a learning opportunity. Although Mo felt appropriately challenged in his work, he rarely felt anxious or bored. He never felt self-conscious or anxious of being judged because Joe had a way of reframing Mo's mistakes or experimental failures as opportunities to learn. Mo never felt conscious of being judged.

Mo realized that succeeding in his leadership role meant he would need to create the kind of positive environment that Joe had done years before. Mo wanted to be a leader like Joe and give his staff a chance to be innovative and creative. Mo committed to leading in this style but recognized this would only be a starting point for creating a positive environment. In addition to modifying his leadership style, he needed to create a positive environment that would minimize "drama."

Mo formed a committee of senior leaders who would make decisions about which IT projects to support and fund. This committee was an important part of the governance of the organization. Mo was aware that his staff had a lot more good ideas than could be funded, so he needed the committee's executive support to identify which projects to bet on. The committee appeared, to some, like a process that entrepreneurs go through to seek funding from venture capitalists.

The aim of the committee was not to micromanage the projects but to set challenging goals for the teams of scientists. The committee also set standards for project milestones and what the milestones needed to accomplish for teams to be successful. Thus, the committee would help scientists determine the outcome needed for further funding and progression.

Mo realized that his leadership team and committee could have a negative impact if they did not behave in a way that focused on how the process would flow. So, he worked with his team and the committee to establish how they would behave during interactions with the scientists.

First, they would set clear goals every step of the way with the scientists. Committee members committed to being available to give scientists immediate feedback on their actions. In addition, the committee committed to getting to know the skills, experience, and capabilities of the scientists.

They determined that a review of a scientist's project would lead to a discussion about the level of challenge of the next steps. This way, the committee could understand if the plans represented a high or low challenge for the scientists and provide the necessary support and resources to optimize skills and challenge of a project.

The committee also agreed to behaving in a way that would encourage the scientists during interactions with the committee. They minimized distractions and disruptions. They gave clear feedback on the priorities for the organization. In the questions and discussions, they had with the scientists, they would minimize the feelings of self-consciousness by creating a less-formal presentation style and make the discussion more open and freer.

They also agreed to not give the impression that they were judging the scientists; they assessed the science, not the person. Furthermore, the committee agreed to frame any scientists' failures as opportunities to learn.

Finally, they created a document detailing their plan and briefly reviewed the document at the start of each meeting.

Mo and his team noticed a difference in the way the whole group worked and realized that their commitment to behave differently had a positive impact.

Mo then put in place the next part of his strategy for creating a positive environment by ensuring diverse and inclusive environment. He knew the value of drawing upon diverse experiences, backgrounds, and ideas. His team's work was to try to solve complex science problems that had not been solved before. He recognized they needed to view the problems with a different lens and diverse perspectives,

Mo knew that diversity was only half the battle, so he established a culture that included everyone. He showed that he was authentic in his belief that he was open to ideas and viewpoints coming from everyone, no matter what the source.

Finally, Mo leveraged his natural empathy to make sure he understood what people needed to be effective. He also lifted his team up through giving feedback, being open, creating a learning culture and celebrating successes (no matter how small).

Chapter Summary

Creating a positive environment is a key factor for successful leadership. A positive environment makes the most of talented people both within and outside the organization. It encourages people to develop and thrive, take advantage of ideas, and develop creative solutions to complex problems.

A positive environment leverages a diverse workforce that feels included, engaged, and motivated to deliver the organization's purpose and strategic goals, whether the group is located in the same office or works virtually across the globe. In a positive environment, people feel the energy in everything they do, and they want to be a part of the outcome as an employee or collaborative partner. There are clear competitive advantages for leaders who create such an environment.

Key Learnings About Creating a Positive Environment

- Energizing, impactful leaders create a positive environment that encourages people to work toward the desired strategic impact and thrive and develop their talent.
- They take advantage of diversity and inclusion to facilitate creativity and innovation to deliver an organization's purpose and strategic goals.
- They create circumstances and conditions that generate positive energy, whether the workforce group is in the same office or works remotely.
- They create an environment where people feel the positive energy in everything they do and want to be part of it.

Action Plan for Improving Your Ability to Create a Positive Environment

In your action plan, take time to reflect on your strengths and your opportunity for growth. This self-reflection has two parts. First, review the following questions and rate yourself for a strength or an opportunity for growth for each question. Next, think about actions that you can take to enhance your strength or develop your opportunity for growth.

1. Do you intentionally plan to create a positive environment?
2. Do you get the most out of your talent and their ideas?
3. Do your group and collaborators feel engaged and motivated around delivering your purpose and strategic goals?
4. Do you encourage and present clear goals and give immediate feedback?
5. Do you intentionally seek to remove distractions and disruptions and reduce uncertainty and unnecessary stress for people around you?
6. Do you set appropriate challenges based on the skills and experience of your staff?
7. Do you frame failure as an opportunity to learn?
8. Do you have an intentional plan to create a diverse and inclusive environment?
9. Do you seek to find common ground first and not focus on differences?
10. When working with a virtual group, do you have an intentional plan to be inclusive?

Chapter 7
Ensuring Effective Decision-Making

"The most difficult thing is the decision to act. The rest is merely tenacity. The fears are paper tigers. You can do anything you decide to do. You can act to change and control your life and the procedure. The process is its own reward."

Amelia Earhart

As a leader, you want to achieve your strategic goals and make a significant impact. Your strategic plan starts with your decisions about what to do and your course of action. Those actions can have a positive or negative impact on what you try to achieve and on your success as a leader. Therefore, effective decision-making is a crucial skill you must develop.

Other people in your organization perceive your actions as your leadership style, and that includes the way you make decisions. For example, if you tend to make decisions by yourself with little consultation with others, and your actions are to tell your staff what they should do, people will perceive you as being authoritarian and very directive. On the other hand, if you make decisions through consultation and finding consensus with everyone in your organization and involve everyone in taking actions, they will perceive your leadership style as trying to connect with everyone's viewpoints.

Understanding yourself is a constant journey. Through reflection, you can appreciate your leadership style, biases, and tendency toward empathizing with feelings of others. These characteristics are important drivers in your decision-making and actions.

I use the term "action" in the broadest sense. An action can be something that a person does physically (even in a virtual setting) or a behavior that a person exhibits. An action can be large in scope and size (a sustained set of actions over a long period of time and involving a large number of people working together). Or it may be an individual action that is short term.

The outcome of an action is that something is different than before the action. In other words, there is a consequence to an action. The consequences of an action can be intentional or unintentional by the person implementing the action and may or may not be under that person's control.

This chapter discusses how leaders can successfully implement their strategy through key actions.

Stages and Consequences of Actions

We can define four stages to action and desired consequences.

Stage 1: An action starts with a decision as to what needs to occur and which course of action to take. The first critical part of an action is effective decision-making.

Stage 2: If the action and decision involve more than one person, there is often the need to raise and negotiating conflict. This may involve aligning those affected by the decision or other key stakeholders to take the desired action.

Stage 3: Usually a decision requires that the system will move from its current state to a new desired state. Most actions require the system to change. Energizing, impactful leaders need to be effective at leading this change of state for the actions to have a positive outcome.

Stage 4: The action leads to consequences. If implemented successfully, the action will lead to a measurable positive change in results.

I just described a linear process. But some larger actions can be more complicated and involve several decisions and conflicts and small change steps. It may be that after the measurable change in results, leaders need to take further actions based on those results. Then the four-stage cycle starts again.

What is Effective Decision-Making?

The first part of an action is making a decision. Energizing, impactful leaders have a robust process for making decisions and can balance all the elements that go into making the right decision. They balance speed in making decisions with a level of rigor necessary to make the actions from the decision be implementable. They also have the courage of their convictions to implement decisions, even when the consequences are not always in their favor.

Let us consider an example of a decision that illustrates some of the challenges a leader may face. It is late on Monday morning, and a group of senior staff at a software company meet to decide whether to invest several million dollars on a project. This is not an easy decision, particularly in a time when their budget is limited. These leaders know that funding this project would mean that other deserving projects would not be funded.

The chairman of the decision-making committee is late. This is not the first time this group had to wait for the boss to arrive. They filled the time discussing the fact that it was raining again and, for the people attending from the United Kingdom, the discussion soon turned to England's soccer team going out of the soccer championship over the weekend after another subpar performance.

The boss is running from back-to-back meetings. Some attendees know that the boss is coming from a meeting with the CEO. Eventually the boss arrives, running into the meeting and putting his papers down with a thump.

The presenter starts her proposal, and she was well prepared to present over seventy PowerPoint slides. The boss spots a typographical error a few slides into the presentation and points it out in his usual pedantic way. This makes an already nervous presenter even more tense.

The meeting continues to grow more tense, and the participation of the others around the table diminishes as the meeting becomes more of a back-and-forth dynamic between the boss and the presenter. After a few hours, the decision-makers make a decision.

This illustration may seem familiar to you as an all-too-common set of events. What are the dynamics going on here around decision-making? In a previous chapter, I described elements that can hinder the process of factors flowing to a desired outcome. In the meeting illustration above, the decision-makers and presenters were in a negative environment.

Effective leaders minimize disruptions. They also create and manage positive energy both within the organization and across collaborations. Positive energy is critical to align an organization to deliver a clear vision. In this illustration, the environment did not seem positive. In fact, it was tense because the boss was late and seemed to focus on details that did not have an impact on the decision at hand.

Sometimes, decisions are simple. But often they are complex with no easy answers. Decisions come from a mixture of analytical data that frame options and emotions or mood. In this meeting illustration, the mood and emotions of the decision-makers had an impact on the presentation of the analytical data. The illustration reveals negative dynamics involved in a large, complex decision that would be made by a group of people.

Negative dynamics can also apply to simple decisions made by an individual leader. In making an effective decision as a leader, you must consider several options and decide on a way forward. You need to make the decision at the right time and consider the risk of delaying deciding on a course of action. Sometimes the worst-case scenario is indecision, not doing anything based on not being able to decide what to do. There are occasions when you can delay making a decision so that you can gather more data to make the decision more robust. It is important that you not make a decision too hastily, without the necessary analysis of the options and the consequences of an action.

In any case, an effective decision is one that will result in an implementable course of action. There is little value in making a decision that cannot be implemented or that may result in unintended consequences.

In my experience, leaders should decide following a disciplined robust process that balances rigor with speed, considering short-term and long-term goals. To make an effective decision, a leader should consider multiple alternative options at the outset and not get locked into one course of action too early in the process. The most effective decisions rely on gathering and analyzing information and data to forecast the potential benefits and risks of the decision and subsequent actions.

It is important to involve people that need to be bought into the decision. (I discuss this point more fully later in this chapter.) Finally, an effective decision is one where leaders can measure the impact of the actions to show whether the action achieves the desired impact.

To illustrate effective decision-making, consider this simple example. You plan to have an evening with your family at a local restaurant. The simple decision is which restaurant to choose. The desired action and consequence of this decision is to have an enjoyable meal with your family. The first point is to consider the nature of the restaurant you want to consider—which type of food (Italian, Indian, Mexican, Asian, etc.) and the atmosphere (a formal sit-down meal or relaxed fast food).

It is clear that you need to make a decision now because the family is hungry. The risk of delaying the decision may be that there may be a long wait because the restaurant is busy at this time of day and you probably need a reservation. You formulate several options of where to go. You do not close the options too early, as you want everyone in the family to have input. You are open to suggestions.

You gather data on the different options (online restaurant reviews, past experience, and travel time and distance to the restaurant). You consider which option would result in implementable actions. One restaurant is an hour away from some members of the family, and they would not be able to make it in time. You determine whether everyone knows how to get to the restaurant.

You consider the options based on the short-term objectives of eating sooner rather than later. You also consider the longer-term objective of spending quality time with your family. You consider the benefits of each option to meet your goals. You also consider the risks of each option such as whether the food will taste good at a particular restaurant or whether you will experience slow service.

Finally, you consider who needs to be involved in the decision or at least buy in to the decision. As a family, you consider the options and, through consensus decision-making, you all agree on where to go. The outcome of the decision will be easily measurable, based on whether everyone enjoys the food and atmosphere and has a good time.

The outcome of effective decision-making is a decision that is made at the right time, balances the need for rigor and speed, considers potential benefits and risks of the resulting actions, and considers all available options. Effective decision-making leads to a decision that results in an implementable and measurable course of action that leads to desired consequences.

Selecting the Decision-Maker(s)

Who should be the decision-maker(s)? In my experience, surprisingly, organizations often struggle with this question. It is often unclear who should make a decision and who should be involved in a decision. This lack of clarity can occur whether the decision relates to a large investment or day-to-day smaller decisions.

In some cases, leaders at the top of an organization may want to make all decisions, and there is a lack of empowerment of people lower in the organization. In other cases, no individual is clearly identified to take responsibility for a decision. In this instance, an organization can become mired in endless rounds of discussion to get everyone to agree on a decision. In either of these extreme cases, decision-making can be slow, either waiting for the senior leader to decide or trying to get large numbers of people to agree.

The way organizations make decisions depends on the culture. Is the organization risk averse? Is the culture collaborative, or does it operate on command and control by the senior leadership? Does the organization have a matrix-style hierarchy that dictates levels of decision-making power? Does the organization operate in a cross-functional model where people share information and data that impact decisions?

To illustrate this point concerning culture, clear roles and responsibilities for decision-making consider the following example. Ian was CEO of a company that suffered from the problem of slow decision-making. Decision-making was painful because the way the organization made decisions was by conducting multiple meetings involving many different people from across the organization. The quality of the decisions was good, and there was good alignment of the many stakeholders who were impacted by the decision and were involved in implementing the decision. But the decision-making was slow and complex because the organization had a consensus-driven culture. There was endless discussion to try to find a decision that pleased everyone.

Ian conducted an analysis of all the critical decisions that needed to be made in at this company. He also identified the ultimate decision maker, the individual who was responsible for making decisions. Even though several people needed to be involved in the decision, ultimately there was one individual who was accountable for it.

Ian also identified who needed to provide input into the decision (experts from different functions). These people did not have direct accountability for the decision but had important perspectives on the benefits and risks attached to it.

Then he identified who needed to align around the decision. These were individuals who needed have input to the decision, as they would need to support the implementation and take action from the decision. Finally, he identified who needed to be informed about the decision.

During a series of meetings, Ian and his team clarified and agreed on these various decision-making roles and responsibilities. The impact of this exercise was that everyone involved in the decision-making process knew what was expected of them. By having an individual who was ultimately responsible for a decision, although there might be a lot of discussion about the different options and the pros and cons, one person had to step up and make the decision. Although everyone was not forced to agree with any given decision, they had to support it.

There were some interesting changes in behavior after he implemented this system. As everyone knew their roles and responsibilities, there was less confusion around who would ultimately make the decision. People who had key input into a decision were less likely to lose focus by trying to undermine the decision-maker.

Another change was that discussions were more focused. The best leaders in this environment ensured that they listened to the key stakeholders' and experts' input before jumping to a decision by themselves. They ensured that everyone had the opportunity to input information and feel that their viewpoint was heard. But they knew they would be accountable for the outcome. In other words, they owned the decision.

Finally, there were fewer meetings. There was little point to holding a meeting if the key decision-maker was not in the room. People often attended meetings where the first question was "Who is the decision maker?" If it was unclear who that person was or if that person was not present, there was no reason to meet.

From my experience, effective decision-making requires quality and speed and whether the decisions are strategic in nature or improve day-to-day operations. Decision-making roles and responsibilities affect a company's performance. Effective leaders need to make sure there is no ambiguity over decision rights and the decision-making process.

In today's business world, speed is critical, and ambiguity delays decision-making. Ambiguity around who is responsible for a decision can lead to endless rounds of discussions to try to get everyone to agree. Although there are different roles in decision-making (such as providing information on options or recommending a course of action), there can be no ambiguity around who makes the decision.

The Impact of Emotions in Making a Decision

Earlier, I described the example of a decision as to whether to invest several million dollars on a project and the decision-maker was late to the meeting. This was an important and complex decision. It appeared to be a data-driven decision. The project leader presenting the recommendation for the decision had plenty of data to support making an informed decision.

On one level, although it was a complex decision, it should require thoroughly analyzing the options and the data. But other factors were at play in this meeting: emotions. Some participants were frustrated because the boss was late. Others were in a down mood because of the loss at soccer or the rain. The boss felt some emotions because of the previous meeting with the CEO and the nature of that meeting. Some of his emotions were not easy to switch off, and he had residual feelings from the last meeting that set his mood for the decision-making meeting. These emotions made him lash out at the presenter and her typos in her slides.

His action caused tension and stress that evoked emotions in the presenter including fear, anger, disgust, and anxiety. The impact of these emotions was that she presented her data with less confidence. This was misinterpreted by the others in the meeting and led them to think that she was not confident in her data or her recommendation. The tension between the boss and the presenter also impacted the emotions of the other participants, and some became more reserved and afraid to express their honest opinions on the decision.

Clearly, this is quite an extreme example of the impacts from emotions that arise in a decision-making process. It reminds me of a statement made by W. Edwards Deming, a well-known professor, author, and management consultant: "In God we trust. All others must bring data." The story of the meeting illustrates an important point that decision-makers' emotions and moods influence analytical thinking for the decision. Not everyone is coldly analytical all the time.

Interpretation of data can be biased or clouded by people's emotions. In fact, I would go as far to say that emotions always influence decisions. Therefore, as a leader, you should always be aware of your feelings as well as your emotional preferences and tendencies.

For example, a leader may tend to be overly skeptical, cynical, negative, distrustful, or fault finding. If this is the case, a leader may tend to view decision options negatively or be overly pessimistic about outcomes. This kind of leader may overemphasize the negative risks of a decision and focus on reasons for a course of action to fail and downplay the benefits. On the other hand, a leader may be overly optimistic, agreeable, too trusting, or see the world with rose-colored glasses.

Either of these tendencies may lead to an underestimation of risks of a decision and overemphasize the benefits. The "glass can be half empty and half full."

Remember: If your emotional tendencies lead you to overestimate risks and underestimate benefits, it is valuable to seek opposite viewpoints. Of course, the same applies if you tend to overestimate benefits and underestimate the risks. You also should be aware of whether you are prone to stress, anxiety, inattentive to details, or inconsistent, as all these emotional tendencies can impact your decision-making.

I find that it helps to ask yourself some simple questions when you have a decision to make. Start by asking yourself about the characteristics of the options you are considering: How do you feel about the risks associated with the options? What is your level of certainty about the success of each option? Do you feel there is a high level of ambiguity? What would be the impact of delaying this decision?

Next, ask yourself about the emotions that can stem from interpersonal aspects of the decision. What are the emotional impacts of expected outcomes? What is your current emotional state and mood (anger, anxiety, fear, pride, happiness, sadness)? What is the current emotional state and mood of others involved in the decision?

Then ask yourself two final important questions. How are my tendencies influencing my decision-making? What is the impact of my emotion on the decision?

By asking these questions, a strategic leader can monitor the potential impact of emotions on decisions. It may not change the outcome, but they raise the level of awareness of emotional biases that may be at play.

The Impact of Biases in Making a Decision

People often have inherent biases that may surround a decision. There has been a lot written about cognitive biases, and an internet search will point you to comprehensive lists of biases. Some biases have a bigger influence on decision-making than others. I shed light on these influences in the following discussion highlighting my experiences.

Intuitive thinking incorporates one's biases from past experiences. People tend to rely on their intuition to help them associate known things with new things. The dangers of relying on intuitive thinking in decision-making can be profound. It can lead to making the wrong decision. It also can lead to overconfidence in a course of action that does not fully realize the risks but can lead to unintended negative consequences.

From my experience, many people are unaware that they jump to conclusions because of their biases. For instance, if someone broke your trust in the past, you likely have a bias causing you not to easily trust others. If you experienced a negative situation with your boss in a past job, you likely have a bias toward new bosses. In both these instances, your bias would impact your decision-making that involves someone you are not sure you can trust or someone that may cause you anxiety.

In an earlier chapter, I discussed mindsets and underlying past experiences that can cause people to believe they are superior to others. They may believe they have better skills than others, but the opposite may be true.

For instance, I may think that I am a good artist when I sketch a picture because I like the look of the picture. But if I were to take the time to compare my work with others, I would realize that my sketch is simple and lacks basic perceptions of depth, let alone expertise in sketching. My feeling of superiority (although not realistic) in this example will cause me to have biases in making some decisions.

Biases exist in our intuitive thinking, and they become a dangerous blind spot for system thinking. An earlier chapter pointed out the importance of system thinking as a top skill for energizing, impactful leaders. You likely hear people warn, "We do not know what we don't know." Keep that in mind when you make a decision. You may not know the potential impact of the decision or potential options if you rely just on intuition.

In my experience of being involved in major decisions, I became aware of when biases came into play and had to be avoided. Here are a few examples. When decisions are complex, particularly if there is a high degree of uncertainty and risk, there is a temptation to substitute a simpler question.

For instance, a major financial investment was requested to support a project that required an investment over several years. Decision-makers had to consider the chances of success of this long-term investment but equally had to consider the other projects that consequently would not be funded over that time frame.

When multiple high-risk projects are in the portfolio, it is complex to decide which projects to back. No one wants to be remembered for missing out on a highly beneficial opportunity because they backed the wrong horse. In my experience, the most difficult decisions are deciding which high-risk opportunities not to back as much as deciding which ones to back.

This complex set of portfolio decisions may be difficult to think about in the long term. The difficult question of whether to fund a project aggressively for the next five years may be substituted with an easier question of whether to partially fund a project for the next year. Shifting to a short-term decision may not necessarily be a bad decision, but it should be a conscious decision and not a result of bias. "Kicking the can down the road" could be a good thing if getting more data is required to support a longer-term goal.

We all make mental shortcuts in our thought process. Those shortcuts can inadvertently lead to biases in decision-making. A study of psychology reveals several mental shortcuts, such as the "affect heuristic "and the "availability heuristic."

I see instances of the "affect heuristic" in leaders having "pet" projects. A project may be a leader's favorite project because it addresses an issue that is close to the leader's heart. Or the leader may perceive a project as important for the organization. What is the danger in this kind of thinking? If you, as a leader, base your decisions on this kind of thinking, you hope a project will be successful even if data show that it may be a "dog." If you perceive that a project's success will be viewed as a critical part of your organization's success, it may bias your decision-making.

Emotions may get the better of leaders in their decision-making without clear pushback from others with a different point of view. Recalling an old fairy tale, sometimes people must tell the "emperor" he "has no clothes."

Two other situations relate to this point. The first is the concept of "sunk" costs. I see leaders making decisions based on sunk costs. They think, "We already sunk millions of dollars in this project and do not want to lose what we already spent." This colors the view of decision-makers who feel they need to justify the investments they already authorized.

The second concept is "group think." I see organizations where a group of people typically make decisions on investment and, over time, think alike when it comes to new investment decisions. It often takes an outsider from the group to point out that there are other perspectives and that the group members are biased by each other.

In addition to the mental shortcut of the "affect heuristic" described above, another mental shortcut can bias complex decision-making: the "availability heuristic." In some important decisions, one's memory can be short, particularly when decision groups or leaders are new to a role. People may decide on an approach to a problem based on what they tried in the past. The immediate available information can bias a decision if the decision-maker does not consider the experience of the past.

It is possible that something did not work in the past, but the experience of that failure may not be immediately available. A leader may not be aware of past failures. Or the leader may think that the outcome will be different this time around. A "devil's advocate" in the group should ask this question: "We tried this before, and it did not work. Why should the outcome be different today?"

Not considering past experiences may be a result of turnover leaders in an organization that lacks documentation of results to add to institutional memory. In my experience, this was an unintended consequence a trend some years ago of de-layering, taking out middle management and their institutional memory.

Narrative fallacies are another set of potential biases I see in decision-making. We make assumptions about decisions and why we made them in the past. For example, when a major project comes forward for a decision about an investment for the first time, leaders make assumptions about the risks and benefits. It may be clear from this first request that this project has a relatively small probability of success but, if successful, the outcome would have a huge benefit. The decision-makers recognize that this project is worth some investment but know that it is a long shot.

When the project returns for a second investment, the risks are still large, but a small amount of progress was made. The presenters giving information for the decision build a narrative around the success and the potential outcomes. By the time of a request for a third, and larger, investment, the project is still a long shot but the narrative around success drives the decision. Decision-makers agree to the large investment. Three years into the project, it fails to show that it works.

In this illustration, the narrative of success led to decision-makers being biased and forgetting that this was a high-risk project based only on assumptions in the first decision. Most leaders are not good at documenting assumptions during the decision-making process. A narrative, such as success, can bias the decision by not taking the risks into account. Although each decision point in this example should start from square one in the analysis, it was biased by a narrative that continued building, and everyone agreed with that narrative.

I heard anecdotally of a large corporation that developed technologies and became enamored with its technology and the narrative they developed about how good the technology was. They were surprised when customers did not buy it. Those decision-makers were so biased by their assumptions that someone said, "If the customers don't like our solutions, they must have the wrong problems."

Another bias I see in decision-making is over-reliance on experts or pundits. Sometimes experts' opinions may carry more weight in trying to bring some certainty to an uncertain situation. For example, a project team may consult an external "expert" to help with an investment proposal and then quote the expert's opinion in a presentation for an investment decision. This is a valuable approach if the expert has knowledge and experience in the subject at hand and in the organization's context.

If there is an impression that an expert knows more than the organization's decision-makers, this can lead to a bias. The expert may be knowledgeable in a related field but not specifically in the problem at hand. Hence, decisions-makers may give too much weight to that expert opinion. Leaders must take care to understand what an expert brings to the table.

Finally, leaders should be aware of decisions where they are overly optimistic or overconfident. When it comes to project decisions for further investment, most people genuinely want a project to succeed and look for the reasons it will succeed. Conversely, they may not fully appreciate the reasons it may not succeed.

As an example, in the field of drug development, more drugs fail than succeed. This is not always due to bad decision-making; it can be due to unforeseen circumstances that could not be recognized in earlier experiments. In fact, in early phases of drug discovery, more ideas fail than succeed, particularly when ideas are highly innovative and not tried before. This situation calls for as much skill in managing the business of failure as well as success. Over-confidence and inflated optimism may lead to taking more risk of over-promising and under-delivering.

Several factors can influence the decision-making process. Complex decision-making is not always just an analytical exercise. Emotions and biases (conscious or unconscious) can profoundly influence the impact of a decision.

How to Avoid the Influence of Emotions and Biases in Decision-Making

As discussed in a previous chapter, one of the major impacts of being self-aware is being able to trust your intuition. This trust comes from being aware of your emotions and feelings that may be biased based on your state of mind. An appreciation of shifts in your mindset is an important piece of self-awareness. A good example of the negative impact of your state of mind is considering the residual emotions you may carry into an interaction.

For example, you may be in a meeting that is highly emotional, and you discuss issues such as restructuring, which concerns and stresses you. If you leave that meeting and move on to your next meeting, you may carry some of that residual emotion into your next meeting. In a prior illustration, I described the boss who arrived late at a meeting and, for reasons unrelated to the topic, appeared to be overly emotional. He probably brought the residual emotions from his prior meeting.

A best practice I use to overcome this effect is building into my schedule ten minutes between meetings where I can re-center myself emotionally before going to the next meeting. One of the advantages of being aware of your feelings and emotions is that you could monitor this residual effect.

Another way to avoid emotions and biases in your decision-making is being aware of how you are different from others. It is important to know who you are and, equally, to know where you come from. As I explained in a previous chapter, I spend time in my coaching practice discussing with leaders their career, background, experiences, and what influenced the way they frame the world. We also discuss some of the key decisions they made during their career and how and why they made them. This information helps them understand their strengths and biases, which shows them how they make decisions and take action.

Another aspect of being self-aware is knowing how you project your feelings and emotions to other people. You can be aware of this by monitoring the reaction of the other person. A method I use in my coaching business is to take advantage of video conferences as well as face-to-face meetings. In a video conference, you have an opportunity to look at your own image. You can monitor yourself and gain understanding as to of how you project your emotions and feelings.

Part of being self-aware is being aware of your susceptibility to stress. Stress can manifest itself in being moody, volatile, unpredictable, and inconsistent. It also can bring into play other personality traits such as skepticism, being cynical, being overly negative (glass half full), being distrustful, or finding fault. Monitoring and overcoming stress helps avoid these emotions. Otherwise, you risk being over-confident, naïve, or over-optimistic in your decision-making

From a practical perspective, I find it valuable to use a framework to review my emotions and thoughts before I make a major decision. This framework (see the two-part Table below) consists of questions I ask myself before a decision, while making a decision, and once I choose the course of action.

Reflection Question	Potential Actions
Do I fully understand the decision to be made?	If not, get additional information about why, what, when, and how.
Am I clear on what a good outcome from the decision looks like?	If not, visualize what success would look like in both the short term and long term.
Must the decision be made now?	If not, articulate the risks and benefits of waiting. Identify a clear timeline for reconsidering the decision.
Is this a decision that I need to make alone, or should others be involved?	If others should be involved, identify who else should weigh into the decision.
What is my current mood and emotions? Are there incidental influences that stop me from being present for this decision?	If distracted by incidental influences, take a walk, meditate, or use other ways of focusing your mind on the present.
What are the characteristics of the decision that can impact my emotions?	Try to step back from the emotional aspects of the decision. Find additional information that may minimize emotional factors.
Am I overly motivated by self-interest?	Consider the impact of the decision on others who may be affected. Visualize being in someone else's shoes.

Table 1. Decision-Making Framework – Part 1

organized or logical way to find a single answer and make a decision. Convergent thinking involves the group challenging the assumptions of an idea, defining options, and deciding on a course of action. The aim of convergent thinking, as the name suggests, is to focus on a decision and converge on one action.

If you watch a team in action, you usually see a mixture of divergent and convergent thinking at the same time. Some people in the group may want to get to a decision quickly and converge on an action, while others may still want to brainstorm and be divergent. The divergent group is not ready to come to a decision because they feel the group did not yet consider all the options. On the other hand, the convergent thinkers push to get to actions. In a group setting, the convergent group may push hard to a decision that is not necessarily supported by everyone in the group. The group needs to be aware of where they are in the decision-making process.

As a first step for group decision-making, I recommend designing an agenda. I find it valuable to spell out in the agenda what the group aims to do in any given discussion.

As an example, consider an organization that needs a decision on whether to invest in the next round of team activities. The project team reaches several options through divergent thing and presents three options to the governance committee. If the committee is satisfied that the team had a chance to consider many options before deciding on the three to present, the committee's primary function is to converge on the one option to pursue.

Confusion about whether the committee should diverge or converge can be the source of emotions and biases. People trying to converge when the rest of the group is diverging may become frustrated that not everyone gets to a decision. People who try to diverge when the rest of the group tries to converge may become angry that they are shut down or forced into a decision. Again, a facilitator can help the group identify these dynamics and keep the group on track with their decision-making.

skepticism, being cynical, being overly negative (glass half full), being distrustful, or finding fault. Monitoring and overcoming stress helps avoid these emotions. Otherwise, you risk being over-confident, naïve, or over-optimistic in your decision-making

From a practical perspective, I find it valuable to use a framework to review my emotions and thoughts before I make a major decision. This framework (see the two-part Table below) consists of questions I ask myself before a decision, while making a decision, and once I choose the course of action.

Reflection Question	Potential Actions
Do I fully understand the decision to be made?	If not, get additional information about why, what, when, and how.
Am I clear on what a good outcome from the decision looks like?	If not, visualize what success would look like in both the short term and long term.
Must the decision be made now?	If not, articulate the risks and benefits of waiting. Identify a clear timeline for reconsidering the decision.
Is this a decision that I need to make alone, or should others be involved?	If others should be involved, identify who else should weigh into the decision.
What is my current mood and emotions? Are there incidental influences that stop me from being present for this decision?	If distracted by incidental influences, take a walk, meditate, or use other ways of focusing your mind on the present.
What are the characteristics of the decision that can impact my emotions?	Try to step back from the emotional aspects of the decision. Find additional information that may minimize emotional factors.
Am I overly motivated by self-interest?	Consider the impact of the decision on others who may be affected. Visualize being in someone else's shoes.

Table 1. Decision-Making Framework – Part 1

Reflection Question	Potential Actions
Am I in love with one of the options? Have I considered other options equally as the one I favor?	Step back and identify the rationale for that feeling.
Am I giving disproportionate weight to the first information I received?	Consider other information to test those first assumptions.
Am I taking the easy route because I want to avoid potential upheaval of a better, more difficult option?	Get information that will frame the true level of upheaval caused by the more difficult option. Does the benefit outweigh the upheaval?
Am I favoring one option because it justifies previous decisions?	Step back from the decision and consider risks and benefits of other options.
Have I considered looking at the decision in different ways (different framing of questions)?	If not, reframe the decision or look at it from different vantage points.
Am I seeking just information that supports existing instincts or my gut feeling and avoiding contradictory information?	Ask other people's opinions – people you know will not have the same point of view as you.
Am I over-confident or under-confident in the forecasts of the future? Have I considered potential intentional and unintentional consequences of the decision?	Think through what additional information may be needed to strengthen forecasts.

Table 1. Decision-Making Framework - Part 2

This framework helps me stop and reflect before I jump to a conclusion or a quick option. Of course, I can still make bad decisions. But this framework helps raise my level of awareness of potential biases and the impact of my emotions.

How to Avoid Emotions and Biases in Group Decision-Making

The framework illustrated in Table 1 is also applicable for groups making a decision.

The first step for a leader in avoiding the influence of emotions and biases in decision-making is self-awareness; similarly, "group-awareness" is the first step for a group. A future chapter will discuss group dynamics and decision-making in the context of forming "transcendent teams," but there are some points to consider here when looking at avoiding negative impacts of emotions and biases.

The primary way for a group to avoid biases is to be aware of the potential biases that can be part of their process. A discussion of the potential dangers can be a regular part of group meetings. One effective method I see from my career is to have someone in the group assigned the responsibility for facilitating the team interactions and dynamics. This individual can be responsible for highlighting potential biases. The individual also can help to point out to the group when emotions take the group off track and help facilitate defusing these emotions.

The facilitator can be a member of the group who is assigned this responsibility, or someone brought in from outside the group. Both options are effective. However, be aware that this is difficult for individuals who are part of the decision-making, as they may have a biased point of view or may be so involved in the discussion that they cannot step back and observe the dynamics effectively.

It is also helpful for someone in the group to take on the role of a devil's advocate. A key driver of biases in group decisions is that they may suffer from "group think." If the group lacks diversity or if the group worked in harmony for a long period of time, group members may start to bring similar framing to a situation (which is a bias).

A way to avoid this bias is to appoint someone in the group or from outside the group to take a counterview and argue against the recognized set of assumptions. The counterview of a devil's advocate is important to reframe the group's assumptions and to expand their thinking. It is only valuable if this person's views can be heard and if the rest of the group is not closed to devil's advocate's views. I find it valuable to identify the role of devil's advocate so that everyone knows that person's role is to disagree with the group.

Another point to consider regarding avoiding emotions and biases in group decision-making is the concept of divergent and convergent thinking. As explained in a previous chapter, divergent thinking is when a group generates creative ideas and looks at multiple ways to solve a problem. They explore options, are free thinking, and share different views on a solution. They identify possibilities. They brainstorm to get all possible solutions out on the table without analysis or criticism. Ideas are not good or bad in this type of thinking; they just are ideas.

Convergent thinking, on the other hand, puts ideas together in an organized or logical way to find a single answer and make a decision. Convergent thinking involves the group challenging the assumptions of an idea, defining options, and deciding on a course of action. The aim of convergent thinking, as the name suggests, is to focus on a decision and converge on one action.

If you watch a team in action, you usually see a mixture of divergent and convergent thinking at the same time. Some people in the group may want to get to a decision quickly and converge on an action, while others may still want to brainstorm and be divergent. The divergent group is not ready to come to a decision because they feel the group did not yet consider all the options. On the other hand, the convergent thinkers push to get to actions. In a group setting, the convergent group may push hard to a decision that is not necessarily supported by everyone in the group. The group needs to be aware of where they are in the decision-making process.

As a first step for group decision-making, I recommend designing an agenda. I find it valuable to spell out in the agenda what the group aims to do in any given discussion.

As an example, consider an organization that needs a decision on whether to invest in the next round of team activities. The project team reaches several options through divergent thing and presents three options to the governance committee. If the committee is satisfied that the team had a chance to consider many options before deciding on the three to present, the committee's primary function is to converge on the one option to pursue.

Confusion about whether the committee should diverge or converge can be the source of emotions and biases. People trying to converge when the rest of the group is diverging may become frustrated that not everyone gets to a decision. People who try to diverge when the rest of the group tries to converge may become angry that they are shut down or forced into a decision. Again, a facilitator can help the group identify these dynamics and keep the group on track with their decision-making.

ENERGIZE TO IMPACT

Energizing, Impactful Leadership in Action: Effective Decision-Making

Philippe is head of a technical group in a large manufacturing company, his employer for many years. While working on his PhD, he enjoyed research and training in the cutting-edge technologies involved in the production of antibodies. So, it was a natural transition for him to join a start-up biotechnology company that produced antibodies to treat inflammatory diseases such as arthritis and joint pain.

He is a well-respected leader. The first thing people say about Philippe is that he "knows his stuff." He is well liked, and people enjoy working with him. He also assembled a very competent team, and they work well together. His team is successful in delivering his organization's needs, and his senior management recognize that this is primarily due to Philippe's leadership.

Although they are successful, Philippe is aware that they work in a fast-changing, dynamic area of science. There are many advances in the biopharmaceutical manufacturing space, and it is difficult for Philippe and his team to keep up with these advances.

His company also went through a lot of change over the past few years. Changes included changing priorities in the company products due to new management but also due to some failures in the R&D pipeline. These shifting priorities also led to organizational changes. In fact, Philippe had three different managers in the past two years.

At the end of another successful year, Philippe took some time off to recharge his mental batteries and prepare for the coming year. This was a great time for him to spend time with his family and friends and disconnect from the day-to-day schedule. At one of the family parties, he spent time with his brother-in-law, the CEO of a small retail business. They started chatting about their different roles in very different businesses. His brother-in-law asked, "What keeps you up at night?" This was an interesting question for Philippe, and he did not have an immediate answer.

Over the next few days, he reflected on the question and realized what kept him up was not the day-to-day operations of his team or even the constant change. His challenge was not how to be successful but, rather, how he could continue to be successful. He knew that his business constantly changed, and his competitive advantage was his ability to keep ahead of these changes. Philippe knew that for his team to be successful in three years he would need to make decisions now that would be implemented and have an impact in three years. Philippe concluded that now was a key time to make some decisions as to which technologies in which they should invest money and resources. Now was the time to make some strategic decisions to ensure the continued success of his team.

Philippe had some actions to take, and that started with decisions around the direction of his team and his organization. He started by considering the outcome or actions that he wanted to result from the decision: he would have an implementable and measurable improvement to the impact his team had on the business.

Philippe pulled his team together to start the decision-making process. At that meeting, they discussed what a potential future would look like for their business and how the team could impact that future. They discussed several potential actions, and he assigned some team members to define several different options. The organizational culture was very collaborative, and Philippe knew that involving his team in defining these options would be important.

The team mapped out a plan and decided who should recommend a course of action, who needed to agree to the recommendation, who needed input in the decision, and who would be impacted by the decision. Philippe knew that there were several stakeholders, including his manager and his peers, that would need to align with the decision. He defined a plan to define different options that included consultation with his manager and peers. Ultimately, the decision on the direction of the group was his to make; but if it required additional resources, his manager would need to make the decision. The team agreed to meet again to discuss the different options for the future and decide which one they would recommend to his manager.

Philippe was determined to have a robust decision-making process that was based on the analysis of data and that would minimize the effects of emotions and biases. He also wanted a process that would result in actions that were implementable and supported key stakeholders. Most importantly, he wanted a process that would result in decisions and subsequent actions that would have a positive impact on his purpose and strategic goals.

His project teams worked on identifying the necessary decisions and identifying the problems they needed to solve. As part of this process, he decided to ask for the help of a facilitator. The facilitator was not part of his team, so he would not be involved in content discussion. The facilitator also was independent insofar as he had no bias toward one decision or another. The facilitator helped him keep the team on track and constructed "group awareness" agendas for the meetings. He also pointed out when the team converged too early or when the discussion opened (diverging) when something had already been agreed or decided.

Philippe scheduled a series of meetings for his full team that focused purely on strategic decisions. The first two meetings encouraged divergent thinking. The project teams framed the problems to be solved, and the full team brainstormed ideas to solve these problems without the constraints. He did not want to close thinking too early and resisted the temptation to jump to a decision immediately. His role as the leader was to be open to ideas and have no pre-conceived notions. He was careful not to provide his ideas first because he knew that this might stifle the discussion.

During the discussions, he rewarded and praised people who generated novel ideas. He wanted the whole team to be divergent and free thinking about the future.

The result of these meetings was that his team generated more than one hundred and fifty ideas, ranging from new technologies that should be introduced to the group to increase productivity to a range of new skills that needed to be introduced to the team. Philippe was impressed by the open discussion that occurred at the team meetings.

The facilitator stepped in a few times when someone tried to critique an idea and tried to converge on a decision. Philippe actioned sub-teams to take all the ideas that applied to their area and start to develop some options for the next meeting.

Philippe designed the second set of meetings to involve convergent thinking to come to some decision about the options they would pursue and present to his senior leadership. He was aware of his own tendencies when making decisions in that he could be risk adverse when he was stressed or if there was a high level of uncertainty. He knew that his team thought strategically in the meetings and, in their dynamic world, they would forecast a future where there are many unknowns.

He was aware of his tendencies to be overly directive with his team when he was stressed and worked to monitor this behavior in these meetings. Although, he felt uncomfortable in these discussions at the time, he knew that the decisions would be better for the team if he could avoid his biases. The facilitator in these meetings was helpful to point out to him when he became too directive with the team.

The structure of these decision-making meetings was that the project teams would present their ideas and the supporting data for each option so that the whole group could decide which options to pursue. The nature of these decisions was that they would do things differently in the future.

Each option would require a lot of change within Philippe's organization. In some areas, Philippe and his team were clear that they did not want to preserve status quo just because change would be difficult. In some areas, they knew that they had to decide on some difficult changes that could be painful in the short term but would result in longer-term benefit. These changes might result in having to let people go and hire new skills.

These decisions were not short of emotions within the team, which was understandable; but they had to recognize and manage the emotions. Philippe was impressed by his team's maturity in discussing these emotional issues, and they used the available data to help drive their discussions and decision-making. The facilitator helped Philippe navigate the emotional aspects of the meeting. Indeed, at one point in the first meeting, the facilitator called a "time out" to let some participants get their emotions under control. He also gave everyone some time at the start of each meeting to vent any residual emotions they had. He encouraged them to get things off their mind and leave them at the door. Philippe encouraged the team to use unemotional data analysis to understand the benefits and risk of any given option.

Philippe also was aware that because the team was well established and knew each other for a few years, they were prone to "group think." They tended to see issues in a similar way because they had a shared history with the department. Philippe wanted to avoid this phenomenon in the important decisions about their future. He asked one of his peers to join the meetings as a devil's advocate. He knew this person had different views from the rest of his team and would not be afraid to raise counterviews and push back on assumptions.

This strategy worked very well. It was clear from the beginning that the peer was there to have different views, and the team respected the role he played. During the discussions, the team identified a few occasions where they would have agreed on an option very quickly, but the devil's advocate raised some not-yet considered questions.

Finally, Philippe was aware that there were other potential biases that could impact the team's decision-making. He knew some team members already really favored some ideas. With the help of the facilitator, the team established a way of ensuring they accessed the supporting data for each option with the same level of rigor. In a similar way, Philippe used rigorous analysis of available data for each option to be sure that the team was not biased by "sunk costs." from past heavy investments in technology. The team worked hard at these decision meetings to try to create a base line of each idea independent of past investments. The facilitator also helped the team to avoid the fallacy that, because they had been highly successful in the past and continued to be at the time of the meetings, it did not ensure success in the future. Their future was a fast-moving environment that did not ensure success, so they needed to avoid the success-narrative bias and think in an innovative way for the future. The facilitator was an invaluable part of the team and used a checklist of questions to test the team's assumptions and decisions.

Philippe was happy at the end of these meetings because they used a robust decision process to identify the options for future development of his organization, which he could take to his senior leadership. He was happy that they did everything they could to use analytical data and minimize the negative impacts of emotions and biases.

ENERGIZE TO IMPACT

Chapter Summary

Effective decision-making is an important skill for a leader. It is a robust process that balances speed with rigor, involves the right people, and balances analysis while avoiding negative impacts of emotions and biases.

Decision-making requires that a leader have a high degree of self-awareness and, if a group of people are involved in making the decision, a high degree of group awareness.

Effective leaders consider two primary aspects of effective decision-making. First, the decisions need to result in an implementable and measurable course of action that leads to desired consequences. As with all change, measures should be in place to track successful implementation.

Second, once a decision is made, the leader needs to have the courage of his or her convictions. Some decisions are challenging, and the outcome may be painful. But the leader needs to stay the course and implement the decision. Leaders do not do this blindly. Sometimes, it makes sense to change the decision if new data show a different course of action is desirable. Effective leaders do not flip-flop on decisions just because the outcome is hard.

Key Learnings about Effective Decision-Making

- Energizing, impactful leaders are effective in making decisions.
- They use a robust decision-making process that balances speed with rigor, involves the right people, and balances analysis while avoiding negative impacts of emotions and biases.
- Decision-making requires that a leader has a high degree of self-awareness and, if a group of people is involved in making the decision, a high degree of group-awareness.
- This process should result in an implementable and measurable course of action that leads to desired consequences.
- They also have courage of their convictions and follow through on their actions.

Action Plan for Improving in Effective Decision-Making

In your action plan, take time to reflect on your strengths and your opportunity for growth. This self-reflection has two parts. First, review the following questions and rate yourself for a strength or an opportunity for growth for each question. Next, think about actions that you can take to enhance your strength or develop your opportunity for growth.

1. Do you make effective decisions that are implementable and measurable and that lead to actions and desired consequences?
2. Do you involve the right people in a decision?
3. Are you clear about who has ultimate responsibility for decisions?
4. Do you have a high degree of self-awareness of your mood and emotions when making decisions?
5. Do you have a high degree of understanding others' moods and emotions when making decisions?
6. Are you aware of the characteristics of the decision-makers? Do they tend to be overly skeptical, cynical, negative, distrustful, fault finding, prone to stress, inattentive to details, inconsistent, optimistic, or agreeable?
7. Do you identify the characteristics of the options available for a decision that can impact emotions such as a high level of uncertainty or risk?
8. Are you aware of the emotional impacts of expected outcomes of decisions?
9. Are you aware of your potential biases when making decisions?
10. Do you minimize biases by using facilitators and devil's advocates?

Chapter 8
Negotiating Conflict and Leading Change

"Peace is not the absence of conflict, but the ability to cope with it."

Mahatma Gandhi

Strategic actions start with decisions. Decisions often leads to conflict and change. Leading through change and conflict are key skills of energizing, impactful leaders.

During the decision-making process and once a decision is made, leaders need to align the people affected and other key stakeholders to take the desired action. In my experience, it is not uncommon for a leader to find disagreement or disharmony between people or ideas that leads to a clash. This conflict manifests in many ways and may be an open disagreement. At other times of conflict, people may not openly express their differing views. Sometimes, people disagree with a decision and do not express their disagreement until after a decision is made. This is passive disagreement.

In this scenario, the leader may not realize someone has a different view until the organization begins implementing the decision. Passive disagreement often can be more destructive than open disagreement. It is a source of negative energy and can derail an action. It is a common mistake for leaders to think that because people do not openly disagree that they, therefore, agree. Unless there is stated agreement by all parties, there may be individuals who do not agree but just do not state it.

One reason this happens is because people fear conflict with a boss who leads with authoritarian behaviors (as highlighted in a previous chapter discussing mindsets). I experienced this situation firsthand, working with a leader who was very directive in her style. This leader did not want to hear anything that did not agree with her opinion or ideas. She discouraged people from "rocking the boat." She wanted harmony in her team, at all costs, if it was on her terms. It was a risk to be outspoken and raise conflict. As a result, people did not discuss all risks when making decisions. No one wants to hear "I told you so" when things go wrong. However, despite the fact that raising conflict carries risk, raising conflict and negotiating conflict resolution is an important skill for energizing, impactful leaders.

Raising Conflict

What can you do as a leader to encourage people to raise conflict? The previous chapter discussed the value of having people in your decision-making process who bring a counterview to your discussions. These devil's advocates are only effective if leaders allow them to be heard and share their views, even if this leads to conflict within the group. In fact, the role of a devil's advocate is to raise conflict.

Conflict is often a core component of innovation. I pointed out earlier the need for leaders to create an environment that is open to diversity in background, thinking, and experiences. Diversity is only valuable if everyone feels included and their voices are heard. As a leader, you need to make sure everyone's viewpoints are heard, even if those ideas lead to conflict. Conflict is a natural part of diverse thinking in a group, and you must manage it well.

Prior chapters explained the importance of a leader's self-awareness of personal behaviors and how they impact others and the impact on achieving goals. Discussions also focused on the benefits of creating a positive environment that ensures inclusion. Both definitely come into play in the need to raise and manage conflict.

For example, as a leader, if you demonstrate behaviors that others perceive as closed-minded or too directive, this may have the impact of stifling new ideas or micromanaging people, which leads to people feeling disengaged. It is difficult to raise conflict in this case, and people may be afraid to express their concerns and want to avoid the fall-out from arguments.

In contrast, if you demonstrate behaviors that others perceive as being open to other views and ideas and being inclusive, the outcome is that people will be more engaged and be willing to take risks in sharing their views. When you create an open, positive environment, it makes people more comfortable about raising conflict in a positive sense.

It only takes a couple of incidents that are perceived as being negative to destroy the positive environment. In my experience, it takes many more positive experiences to create a positive environment than it does negative ones to create a negative environment.

As an effective leader, you also should monitor your positive presence. If you are open, honest, and authentic, it helps encourage the formation of trust-based relationships. Another important behavior you should exhibit in how you show up is giving the impression that raising conflict is an important part of the thinking process in your interactions and in your team.

Finally, your behavior should clearly signal your approach to failure is an opportunity to learn. An environment where people dread failure or its impact leads to people not taking calculated risks, which will discourage raising conflict.

A key tool involved in creating a culture of raising conflict is to establish ground rules or group norms that recognize that raising conflict is welcome and should be part of everyone's day-to-day interactions. Creating ground rules for your interactions can apply to your individual interactions or group activities. A by-product of spelling out that you welcome conflict and it is an important part of how you work is that you will appear more open to others' views and ideas.

Raising conflict should not be a passive process; invite everyone to raise different perspectives. Avoid the trap that you assume everyone agrees or had an opportunity to provide their views if they are silent.

Silence does not necessarily mean they agree. Maybe they just do not want to disagree. Be proactive and confirm that everyone agrees. This is particularly important in virtual interactions by phone or video. Silence may be due to participants being on mute.

I experience this problem particularly if there is a large team meeting together in one room with others dialing in by phone. There is a danger that the people in the large room will dominate the discussion, and it may be difficult for people on the phone to speak up. It is easier to judge the cadence of the meeting when you can see each person or are part of the large group; it is less easy when you are on the phone. The team, and the leader in particular, should proactively involve everyone.

Earlier in this chapter, I suggested that you identify a member of the team as a facilitator, someone who can monitor the dynamics of the interaction and monitor conflict. An important role for the facilitator is to monitor everyone's involvement in the discussion. The aim of the interaction should be that all potential conflicts are raised and resolved. The desired outcome is not that everyone agrees with a decision but that they are willing to support it after the interaction.

Negotiating and Resolving Conflict

An important trait for an energizing, impactful leader is to manage conflict and come to a positive resolution when conflict occurs. One of the reasons that people often see conflict as a negative situation is their concern that people who raise conflict will risk the relationship they have with their co-workers. Conflict is not just about the content of the disagreement but also about emotions and relationship.

Successful conflict resolution results in agreement on how to proceed with the issue at conflict and proceed in a way that preserves or strengthens the relationship between the parties. Whether the conflict surrounds a large or small issue, the basic dynamics of conflict resolution involve negotiating between two or more parties that have a different perspective. I would argue that a successful leader is highly skilled in negotiations and has a good understanding of negotiating dynamics.

There are a few principles that are valuable for strategic leaders to keep in mind regarding negotiation skills. As I mentioned, the risk that an argument can hurt a relationship is one of the reasons that people do not raise conflict. The principle you need to keep in mind as a leader is that the success of an agreement or resolution of a conflict is not an end in itself. Success comes to an agreement that is actionable and implementable, and there is little value coming to an agreement that you cannot implement.

A good example is when negotiating with a supplier. Your position may be to get the lowest cost you can negotiate for a particular supply, and you may win that battle. But it is of little value if the quality of the product is not up to a standard you need or if the supplier goes out of business. This may be acceptable if this is a one-off transaction. But if you need these supplies for the long term, you need to build a relationship with the supplier and reach a deal that is sustainable for both parties.

In my experience, when people take a position and refuse to budge, it is difficult to get alignment with your team or stakeholders around a decision. Consider the following example that occurred when I led a team. During a team meeting, two team members had very different views on a decision that the team needed to make. Joe disagreed strongly with a suggestion made by Sally, who laid out her view very strongly. Joe held fast to his view and started laying out the case for why he was right and why Sally was wrong. Sally reacted to what she saw as an attack and pushed back on why Joe's suggestion made no sense. Emotions soon become heated and insults flew through the room.

I was happy that the different views were out on the table. These views gave us different perspectives on the same issue. However, Joe and Sally were firm in their positions; so, if they continued to argue with this level of emotions, there was a good chance that they would damage their relationship. The rest of the team sat in silence and shifted uncomfortably in their chairs. They knew they did not want to get in the middle of this fight. I was tempted to step in and support one position and make a decision. But there was a good opportunity to find a solution that considered both viewpoints and solve the problem in a better way. I thought it was time to step up and manage this conflict, negotiate the best solution for the team, and preserve the relationships in the team. It was time for a time-out to diffuse emotions in the room.

When you as a leader find yourself in conflict, it is best to separate the people dynamics from the content of the conflict. You need a well-developed degree of empathy so that you can accurately discern the emotions around a difference of opinion.

For instance, Sally and Joe were passionate about their positions, and emotions started getting in the way of their listening to each other's point of view. I recognized their emotions, validated the emotions, and brought the discussion back to the problem to be solved. I felt the important point was that coming to an agreement around the substance of a negotiation was the primary aim. But I also wanted to preserve the relationship between Joe and Sally and the rest of the team. The heated nature of the discussion would impact their relationship with the team.

I called a time-out to discuss their behavior and how it impacted the work of the team and the ability to solve problems. From this discussion, they realized the importance of their relationship and agreed how they should behave to get to the best resolution of the substance of the discussion. I learned that in a highly emotional one-on-one interaction, it is valuable to step away from a heated issue and discuss how you want the relationship to be preserved even if you disagree with the substance of the discussion.

As a leader, you need to understand the difference between what someone wants to get (interests) and positions that person may take. In the example about the conflict between Joe and Sally, their interests were that they wanted the best solutions for their team to use. They both had an interest in the team being successful. They just had different positions on an issue. It was possible to find a solution since they had shared interests.

One of the roles of a leader is to find shared and compatible interests as a starting point for conflict resolution. In the case of Sally and Joe, they each had strong differing positions, but they both wanted recognition from the leader and fellow team members. As a leader, you may want to keep this point in mind and find ways to give team members recognition for generating ideas, whether you use those ideas or not.

In negotiations to resolve conflict, it is also useful to try to get the parties to compromise. Joe and Sally had two positions in the way forward that they felt were best for the team. Either Sally wins and Joe loses, or vice versa. I worked with them to invent new options that would be a win-win solution for the team and of mutual benefit.

In an earlier chapter, I explained that in group decision-making there is divergent and convergent thinking. Divergent thinking is when teams explore options and are free thinking and share different views on a solution using tools such as brainstorming to get all possible solutions on the table without analysis or criticism. Convergent thinking puts ideas together in an organized or logical way to find a single answer and make a decision. Convergent thinking involves the group challenging assumptions of an idea, defining options, focusing on a decision, and converging on one action. This is similar to negotiation dynamics of opening options through divergent thinking before jumping to a decision.

Sally and Joe wanted to use convergent thinking, closing the thinking because they both felt one was right and the other was wrong. The conflict occurred because they had move to convergent thinking while the team was in divergent-thinking mode to get ideas out on the table. As the leader, I could take them back to divergent thinking and ensure all the potential options were on the table. I could then define the process by which convergent thinking would occur and a decision would be made for the mutual benefit of Sally, Joe, and the whole team. This re-framing of the interaction helped get back to understanding their interests and move them away from a pre-judged position.

As the leader, you must ensure objectivity in negotiation conflict. I worked with Sally and Joe to agree a fair set of standards that defined the resolution of their conflict. Their difference of opinion was based on which company they wanted to use to develop a software package. They each had a preferred company based on their experience. In the meeting with the team, they laid out their reasons for wanting to use their preferred company. As the leader, I facilitated the resolution to this conflict by defining standards of price, quality, and time to develop the software. There are some standards that the team used before in making a similar decision, and I used that experience to define a set of objective criteria for deciding which company to use.

Sally and Joe had a shared interest in getting the best developer at a reasonable price, who could provide a timely and quality product. They agreed on criteria and standards we needed from a supplier. They also agreed that there would be an independent assessment of both companies against these standards and that the data would drive the decision.

The team also identified a third company, which was not the choice of Sally or Joe. This company measured well against the criteria and out-performed Sally and Joe's choices and won the contract. The lesson for the team was that it was important to raise the different ideas, as this led to a new option that was best for everyone involved. Conflict and conflict resolution through negotiation played an important part in the successful outcome.

Energizing, Impactful Leadership and Negotiating Conflict

As a leader, you have an opportunity to create energy in others by the way you handle conflict. Positive energy results from being open to other views and ideas, even if it leads to conflict. Once conflict occurs, you can generate positive energy by using negotiating skills to find a solution to the conflict. Bear in mind that negative energy can result from stifling other views because you are concerned about conflict causing disharmony or bad feelings.

The ability to resolve conflict and negotiate solutions to problems is a critical skill for energizing, impactful leaders. Making decisions on actions to deliver purpose and strategic goals often involves getting the support of key stakeholders and partners. Negotiating conflict with the focus on solving differences and preserving relationships will lead to alignment around decisions now and in the future.

ENERGIZE TO IMPACT

Eight Aspects of Dealing with Conflict

To be an effective leader, I believe you need to frame your thinking and actions around eight primary aspects when dealing with conflict. First, conflict is a significant piece of creativity. View conflict as a way of thinking rather than something you should avoid or fear. There are bigger dangers in not raising conflict and keeping issues hidden than you could encounter in a well-managed conflict-resolution process. If you create your positive environment with appropriate handline of conflict, others will see it as a natural part of the process and reward and celebrate it.

The second aspect is how you manage your positive presence. You need to be aware of the impact of your behavior on others. This involves intentionally acting, communicating, and listening to others. It involves building and managing trust in relationships and being authentic (attuned to their most sincere selves even under stress). Finally, it involves your being present in the moment.

Third, resolving conflict in a positive way that is mutually beneficial to everyone is a skill that can have a major impact on your success or failure in delivering your purpose and strategic goals. Take a disciplined approach to how you negotiate conflict.

Fourth, leading a conflict-negotiation process requires a high degree of self-awareness, empathy, and having an open mindset. In other words, you know your strengths and weaknesses, you identify your emotions and feelings, and you have a desire to learn, including learning from criticism and embracing challenge. It also requires a high level of self-control and focus on goals without being distracted.

In addition, you need to be empathetic to others, understanding their perspectives, feeling what they feel, and having a good sense of what they need.

Fifth, you should avoid negotiating around positions people take to resolve conflict. Instead, focus on understanding the real needs of all parties and their stakeholders.

A sixth factor to keep in mind is the desired outcome. Negotiating conflict resolution should focus on resolving the substantive issue and building and preserving relationships. When relationship issues occur, you should deal with them separately from issues associated with the substance of the discussion. Relationship issues often arise from emotions, perceptions, or communication, which you need to manage.

Also, resist an outcome of agreeing to short-term gains that may hurt a sustainable relationship; do not agree just to preserve harmony in a relationship.

The seventh factor for framing your conflict negotiation approach is that you should invent options that result in gains for everyone and focus on strategic goals. This requires differentiating divergent from convergent thinking, not jumping to judgment too quickly, not searching for a single answer, and not assuming that the pie percentages are fixed. Accept that you cannot meet everybody's interests one hundred percent. Compromise when necessary, but not at the cost of the overall purpose and goals. Stay focused on the critical goals and objectives.

Finally, when resolving a conflict, define a set of criteria that involves fair standards and a fair process. Separate emotions and biases when applying the criteria, and do not yield to pressure. Keep the discussion focused on a bigger perspective.

Leading Change

Most decisions require that the system will move from a current state to a new desired state. As you move toward your vision and achieve strategic goals, your system will change. To have a positive impact, you need to be effective at leading this change of state.

Of course, leading change starts with defining the vision. As discussed in an earlier chapter, you must understand the current system so that you can analyze the gap between the current and future desired state. As the leader, you will be responsible for generating roles and responsibilities for the change effort as well as the action plans enabling the shift from the old to the new state. Naturally, the next step is to implement the plans.

Highly effective leaders recognize they need to measure and monitor the progress of the actions and the outcome of change. Make sure your measurements align with the definition of "success" in the vision. Finally, your effectiveness needs to include documenting and building your new approaches into business as usual. Let us explore these steps for leading change in more detail.

Defining the Vision

As explained in an earlier chapter, a key skill for energizing, impactful leaders is strategic thinking. You must know your purpose, as it helps create energy. You then develop strategic goals and inspire others to follow.

Your vision should be inspirational and engaging and a vision that people can get behind. It also should articulate what the future state will look like. For instance, in my coaching practice, I often ask," If we are successful in one year after you change behaviors you want to develop, what would that success look like?" Defining success helps to set a direction for the change effort.

Your vision for a change effort needs to create a sense of urgency. In other words, why does the change need to happen now? A sense of urgency will help to drive the pace of change and create energy around the vision. People are more likely to change the way they work if they see a clear benefit or a threat.

For example, changing the way you develop a product that would require reorganizing your sales and marketing team may be a difficult and painful exercise. If the vision is that this change will result in the product becoming available to more customers, this represents a clear benefit. If by acting now you will make a valuable product available sooner to customers in need, this is a beneficial reason to act now. On the other hand, if a competitor is about to launch a similar product and you need to change to get to market first, then the situation is urgent due to the threat of the competition. In either case, part of defining a vision for a change is to create a sense of urgency and a reason to act now.

When creating powerful strategic goals, make sure they align with the overall vision you want to achieve. Before making a decision on which actions to take, think through what want to achieve and define what success would look like for the action.

Understanding the Current System

Energizing, impactful leaders are system thinkers. They analyze the system of which they are part and frame their strategic plans and actions in the context of the whole system rather than individual parts. As explained in an earlier chapter, system thinking involves understanding the internal and external environments and recognizing patterns, trends, challenges, interconnections, and interactions in their system. Analyzing the current system involves understanding organizational climate, organizational characteristics, organizational culture, formal and informal structures, and individual and organizational readiness for change.

Most change efforts do not start with a blank slate. I see change efforts that prove to be challenging because leaders underestimated the complexity of the current situation. Not only can this lead to barriers to change, but it also can result in unintended consequences.

As an example, put yourself into the situation referred to above. The vision is to develop a new product to get to market sooner than your competition, which requires reorganizing the marketing and sales organization. As you analyze the current system, you find that the people with experience in this market are not part of your organization.

If you change your organization, you may impact people in another group who are working on another product in that market. If you change your organization, you may cause a negative impact on another part of the company. This may not change your decision, but it will change how you implement your decision. Even if your change is relatively small in scope, it is worth understanding the starting point for change effort.

Analyzing the Gap Between the Current and Future State

Once you have a clear vision for the future state you aim for and a good understanding of your current system, you need to analyze the gaps. What changes are necessary to achieve the desired effect? These changes can involve different elements in your system such as processes, technology, leadership, or decision-making. The decision also may require changes in your organizational climate, culture, or organizational structure.

Delivering on your vision may require pulling multiple levers. For instance, introducing a new technology solution may not be as simple as training people on how to use the technology. It may also require that the process that generates data may need to change, or a leader's decision-making behavior may need to change.

In my career, I saw a new database introduced into an organization to track resources and projects. It was only partially successful because senior leaders did not use the data from this system in making their priority decisions. Project managers still used their own systems of tracking projects outside the new technology and used these data when presenting to senior leaders. For the database to be successful, the change leader needed to pull several levers including changing leaders' decision-making processes.

The output from this stage of the change process is a clear plan of what needs to change to deliver on the vision.

Generating Roles and Responsibilities for Change Effort

The next step is to identify who will be involved in the change effort. First, identify a person or group of people who will guide the implementation. This sponsorship group is usually the leader(s) who has responsibility for the action and the resources needed to implement the change. If the action is within a group, this sponsor is the most senior person. Change involving more than one group requires a powerful guiding coalition of sponsors.

The role of the sponsor(s) is to show commitment to the change and communicate the vision and strategic goals. Sponsors also may have a key role in approving change designs and keeping track of the impact of the change.

Depending on the scale of the desired change, there may be a need to bring together individuals to help design what the change will look like. These design teams are tasked to work on a piece of the change effort and make recommendations to the sponsor.

In the example of speeding up the development of a new product, the sponsor may be the head of research and development, head of sales, head of marketing, the CEO, or a coalition of these senior leaders. They may commission design teams to propose a new structure for the sales and marketing groups and the associated processes. People familiar with the operation comprise the design teams. Confidentiality at this stage is important, as some changes may have a big impact on the group as a whole.

The third role in this change structure is change leaders. These individuals' task is to identify change plans including communication strategies, training needs, and other issues. They also identify people within the affected group who will help the leaders implement change plans.

In any change effort, there are people who are enthusiastic about change. But many (in varying degrees) will resist change. One role of a strategic leader is to identify the people who will act as change agents, even if the proposed change is limited in scope.

Defining Action Plans to Shift from Old to New

The next step is to define action plans that will shift the organization from the current state to the new desired state. These plans may be tactical in nature and should include preparing the organization for the change. For the change effort to succeed, people will need to end the way they work, transition to a new way of working, and start working in the new way. The plans need to incorporate these steps.

Giving up the status quo and the way people were working and embracing the new way of working can be highly emotional for some people. They may feel fear, unfamiliarity, uncertainty, self-doubt, and apprehension. An important component of an action plan is how to address these emotional concerns.

Some changes will require a cultural change, and transparency and regular communication is key here. Leaders need to regularly communicate the vision and articulate how the future state will benefit the group, be clear about why the change needs to happen, and explain why it needs to happen now. People may be able to accept a series of small changes rather than one big change all at once.

A good action plan prepares people to build resilience and individual readiness for change. If the change leader fails to address these people elements, a natural reaction may be that people resist the change and the implementation will fail.

Another important component of an action plan is building short-term wins. This is particularly true if the change is large in scale and there may be doubt about its success. Achieving short-term wins has two advantages. First, if people see some success, it builds overall momentum for the change. Seeing early positive results helps to get more people on board with the change.

Change agents often generate the short-term wins, as they are willing to take the risk of doing things in the new way. Success breeds success: once there is momentum for the change, fewer people will resist. Early success creates role models of people who are using the new way of working. Leaders can point to these role models as the way forward.

It is also valuable to include in the action plan a plan to consolidate improvement and stabilize the organization. When short-term wins occur, be clear about lessons learned from these experiences and how the organization can continue to build on these successes. This is particularly true if the change requires changes to leadership behavior. Preparing leaders to change their behavior, learn from their experience, and plan to consolidate the benefits of the new behaviors is a key part of the change process.

As an effective leader, you help develop these action plans and ensure that all the necessary components are part of the plans. You also will track the progress of these plans during implementation. No matter the size of a decision and associated actions, it is valuable to think through the action-planning phase and ensure you have plans to implement the decision.

Implementing Action Plans

Implementation of the action plans can come in many forms. It may be that individuals will implement the plans or components of the plans. There also may be the need to form implementation teams that are responsible for implementing the plan. For instance, the leader may assign the HR team to implement new HR practices that align reward and performance systems to the new desired state.

As the leader, you should continuously and consistently communicate the reason for the change, the vision, and purpose of the new desired state. You should communicate what needs to be done to achieve the strategic goals including timelines and transition plans. You do not necessarily need to dictate how people should work. The more responsibility people have in how they work, the higher the level of motivation and engagement they will have.

Change requires that the old way of working will end, and after a transition period, a new beginning will occur. The transition period may be short if the change is small in scope. It may be longer if the change is large. For instance, there may be a project that is near completion that may be "grandfathered" into finishing under the old way of working.

The outcome of this phase is that the decision, action, and change will be built into the new "business as usual" operations.

Measuring and Monitoring Change

During the implementation of a decision that leads to change, you need to measure and track progress toward achieving the goal. You can monitor each part of the action plan for what is working well, and the lessons learned from the implementation.

You can modify plans based on the initial implementation feedback. This also applies to monitoring individual's journeys through the change. You can reduce their stress and organizational stress through clarification and communication. Initial implementation and continued monitoring also can test new thinking.

You should empower others to act. As they come to own the new desired state, they can accelerate the change through their own actions. A key role in your leadership in this phase is to share what people learn and share success stories as they occur. You should track progress and assess success of delivering on purpose, vision, and strategic goals.

Building New Approaches Into The Way You Work

The final step in the process of leading during change is to build the new approaches into the way you work by consolidating improvements and drive for more change. As you reach the new state, embed changes, and maintain progress. You can embed changes by updating standard operating procedures, other workflow documents, and training manuals. As the new state becomes "business as usual," you can adjust things that do not work as planned or needed.

By following the process described above, you can deliver on your strategy and vision, moving the system from a current state to a new desired state.

CHARLES S. DORMER

Energizing, Impactful Leadership in Action: Negotiating Conflict and Leading Change

To keep up with a fast-moving, dynamic environment, Philippe worked with his team to define a strategy for his successful organization. He established a robust decision-making process to identify the new technologies in which they should invest. He encouraged divergent thinking around the available options and, with his team, converged on some key decisions.

During this process, he was aware that some of the decisions were controversial and would affect many different stakeholders. He knew that not everyone would agree with the final decision, and he had a nagging concern that he would not be able to implement the decisions effectively unless there was broad support for the way forward.

Philippe wanted to set up an environment with his team and their stakeholders that would encourage raising and managing conflict. He also wanted conflict to be viewed as a positive way of creating energy around their ideas. Philippe pondered two questions. How could he create an environment in which his team could freely raise conflict? How could he resolve conflict resulting in a positive outcome?

As Philippe thought about implementing the decisions they made, he knew that one decision would be particularly controversial with one of the key stakeholders. He knew this stakeholder needed to be on board for the strategy to be successful. He decided to meet this issue head on and arranged to meet with the stakeholder.

He prepared himself for the meeting and thought about how he could resolve any conflicts that were raised so both could feel they gained from the discussion. The stakeholder's different views might strengthen their strategy and might raise new issues for the team to consider. He concluded that this discussion was an opportunity rather than a threat.

Philippe started the discussion with the stakeholder by setting an expectation: he was looking for input to their ideas and he valued the stakeholder's perspective. He set an expectation that, if they had differences, they would talk them through and resolve any issues as partners.

Not long into the meeting, a conflict arose around a particular piece of the strategy that directly impacted the stakeholder. This was the time that Philippe needed to closely monitor his own behavior and not rush to take a position. He listened carefully to the stakeholder's concerns. He kept his cool and did not immediately react. The stakeholder was aggressively passionate about his views. Philippe discussed with the stakeholder how important their relationship was to their past success and how important it would be in the future. The stakeholder agreed. They agreed that no matter how passionate they were about their ideas; they would listen to each other and preserve their relationship.

Philippe resisted taking up a positional approach and tried to understand where the stakeholder was coming from in his views and his interests when it came to the decision they discussed. The stakeholder's major concern was that, if Philippe's team implemented their decision, he might not get the support from Philippe that he enjoyed in the past. This was a valid concern. Philippe could appreciate that the stakeholder felt threatened by the new strategy, and his aggression was based on a fear of not being able to do his job effectively.

Philippe and the stakeholder asked themselves what options about implementing the new strategy would be of mutual gain. They brainstormed ideas together and practiced divergent thinking together. Philippe started from a point of not having one answer but expanded the possible options that would satisfy his interests in pursuing his new strategy but at the same time meet the needs of the stakeholder. As they considered the options they defined, they also discussed objective criteria they could use to resolve their differences. In this way, they separated emotions and biases from the options they considered.

During the discussion, Philippe kept bringing the discussion back to the overall strategy both wanted to achieve. They both wanted the company to do well and make the best decision to position the company for the future in its dynamic environment. They identified a solution to their differences that met both of their needs.

Philippe was surprised that the solution they came up with was even better than the original proposal. He agreed to provide the support to the stakeholder in several key areas; in return, the stakeholder agreed to provide resources for his new idea. Philippe was comfortable with this compromise, as it did not impact the bigger goals he had for his team and made the strategy easier to implement.

Philippe and his team knew that if they were to achieve the strategy they defined, they would need to lead a change effort in his organization. This decision meant that they would combine two of their laboratories into one and develop a technology laboratory that was new to his company.

When he assessed competitors, he found out that other companies were developing the new technology. If Philippe's company did not build this competency, it would be behind when it came to new products. He also knew that his laboratories needed to deliver their data more quickly than in the past. By combining two laboratories, they could be more efficient.

His vision was clear: his group needed to increase their technical capabilities and generate data more quickly to provide patients with the products they needed. This was a major change that needed to happen as soon as possible. If they failed to make the change, they would soon be behind their competitors; so, there was a sense of urgency.

He set the strategic goals: first, that they would have the new lab up and running by the end of the year and, second, that they would halve the time to generate data from the combined lab within the next twelve months.

He wanted to understand the extent of the change for his organization. Looking at his current organization, it was clear that becoming more efficient by combining the laboratories was the easier goal. They had the skills and the technologies to make this happen, but they needed to restructure the staff and improve the process by which they generated data. The major challenge was that people in the laboratory were set in their ways and might not react well to doing things differently.

The new competency was more challenging, and the organization lacked the necessary new skills. So, they would need to retrain some employees and bring some new people in. They would also need to buy new equipment and modify the laboratory space. They would need to build some new relationships with other departments in the company and form some collaborations with academic laboratories with experience in the new techniques. He worked with his team, and they all agreed on the major gaps and the change drivers.

Philippe and his leadership team would act as the sponsors for this change initiative. They also identified several people in the organization who were open to change and were excited by taking on something new. He recruited these individuals as change agents and early adopters of the change.

He commissioned three design teams for the change. One team would put together a design for the new combined lab. A second team would design the new technology competence. A third team would work out the HR issues including reorganization and building change readiness, financial requirements, and communication strategy. The teams included the laboratory directors and the change agents they identified. The three teams would report to the leadership team and come back to the team with clear action plans for the change to occur. The teams also would identify some opportunities in the next few months for short-term gains. There was a new project that needed to apply the new technology, and this would be a good test case to pilot the new competence.

Philippe and his leadership team met regularly with the design teams. They agreed that there would be an announcement to the whole department outlining the vision, reason for the changes, ideas for the new design, and a clear action plan of when the changes would take effect. Philippe organized a meeting of his staff and presented the plan. He gave a lot of time for questions. There also was a series of meetings where his leadership team met with their staff to discuss the change plan.

They collected people's concerns, and everyone had the opportunity to express their views. There were some concerns about whether this was a good idea and how the changes would affect some individuals; but there was a widespread view that this was a good idea, and people felt that they had been heard.

Philippe and his team had regular staff meetings to give updates on the progress of the change effort, and this gave him an opportunity to monitor the progress of the changes.

As the implementation progressed, there were some early wins. One project in the combined laboratory found a way to cut the data-generation time in half. Philippe was excited by this work, as it proved that they could meet the new timelines. The new lab took some time to get up and running, but it was clear from the early data generated from that lab that this new technology would provide some very useful data that they previously lacked. One of the change agents led that early work and demonstrated some new insights on her project. The vision of the future state started to materialize.

As implementation of the changes progressed, Philippe and his team had regular updates and were particularly interested in the lessons learned. Based on those lessons, they made even more change through a continuous-improvement program. They established what they wanted to achieve, and the new approaches were now well accepted and new processes, techniques, and ways of working were built into their standard operating procedures and training programs. Philippe was satisfied with the changes. He felt proud of his group and what they achieved. He also knew that he had a team that was open and ready for change in the future.

ENERGIZE TO IMPACT

Chapter Summary

Leaders create energy in others by the way they handle conflict. Positive energy results from being open to other views and ideas even if it leads to conflict. Conflict is a significant piece of creativity and should be viewed as a way of thinking and should not be avoided or feared. There are bigger dangers in not raising conflict and keeping issues hidden than can be encountered in a well-managed conflict-resolution process.

Once conflict occurs, positive energy can be generated by the leader using negotiating skills to find a solution to the conflict. The ability to resolve conflict and negotiate solutions to problems is a critical skill for energizing, impactful leaders. It involves intentionally acting, communicating, listening to others, and building trust. Negotiating conflict with the focus on solving differences and preserving relationships will lead to alignment around decisions now and in the future.

When dealing with conflict, a leader should invent options that will result in gains for everyone and options that focus on strategic goals. Compromise when necessary, but not at the cost of the overall purpose and goals. Stay focused on the critical goals and objectives. Use objective criteria to maintain fair standards and a fair process. Keep the discussion focused on a bigger perspective.

A critical skill for energizing, impactful leaders is leading change to achieve purpose and strategic goals. Leaders follow a rigorous process for managing change including defining a vision, creating change roles and responsibilities, action planning, managing implementation, and building new approaches into business as usual.

Key Learnings About Raising and Negotiating Conflict

- Energizing, impactful leaders regard conflict as a positive way of thinking and source of creativity.
- They create an environment where people are not afraid to raise issues because it may cause conflict.
- They create an environment to encourage conflict resolution

that separates positions from interests.
- They use negotiation skills to reach agreements that are mutually beneficial and align with purpose and goals.
- They separate substance from relationships.
- They invent multiple options and use objective criteria to resolve conflict.

Key Learnings About Leading Change

- Energizing, impactful leaders are effective at leading change.
- They know how to lead change to deliver on their vision and strategy.
- They follow a process for managing change that includes defining a vision. They understand their current system and future-state gaps, define change roles and responsibilities, develop action plans, manage implementation including short-term wins, measure, and monitor change, and build new approaches into business as usual.

ENERGIZE TO IMPACT

Action Plan for Improving Negotiating Conflict and Leading Change

In your action plan, take time to reflect on your strengths and your opportunity for growth. This self-reflection has two parts. First, review the following questions and rate yourself for a strength or an opportunity for growth for each question. Next, think about actions that you can take to enhance your strength or develop your opportunity for growth.

1. Do you view conflict as a way of thinking that is important to creativity?
2. Do you create an environment as a leader (listening, communicating, behaving) so that people can raise and resolve conflict?
3. Do you resolve conflict in a way that brings agreement to substance issues and preserves relationships?
4. In a conflict situation, can you invent multiple options and define objective criteria for resolving conflict?
5. In a conflict situation, can you compromise but not lose your overall purpose and goals?
6. How effective are you at defining a clear vision and a sense of urgency for change?
7. Can you identify key gaps and prioritize needs for change?
8. Can you define a clear action plan to shift from the old to the new state?
9. Do you have a process for measuring and monitoring the impact of change?
10. Do you build new approaches into business as usual and continuously improve your organization?

Chapter 9
Leading Transcendent Teams

"We must also keep in mind that discoveries are usually not made by one man alone, but that many brains and many hands are needed before a discovery is made for which one man receives the credit."

Henry E. Sigerist
(A History of Medicine)

In today's connected world, impactful results and actions rarely come from one individual; they involve groups of people. How these groups are organized depends on the task they try to achieve.

They may be groups that are formed to work together for a short period of time to deliver a task. For example, think about a group of volunteers who come together to organize a fund-raising event or gala. They have a specific aim in mind that requires that they work together for the time of the event. They are a group of individuals, each with their own skills, who are loosely organized for a short period until the event is over.

Other groups may be involved in longer-term endeavors that involve delivering a more complex project. For example, a group may be tasked to lead a complex organization and will act as a leadership team. Each member of that group will have responsibility for one piece of the organization and will work together to ensure that the system as a whole aligns around strategies and tasks.

Finally, a third type of group comes together to seek creative solutions to complex problems. Think of the group that came together in the movie "Apollo 13" to solve the problem of how to reduce carbon dioxide levels in the stricken spacecraft. Although they did not remain as a group for long, they had to work as a creative team to solve the problem.

In each of these examples, there is a need to work together for the greater good and to deliver a specific set of tasks. Each can be described as a team bringing together individuals with different skills. Although the team organization is different in formality and duration, there is value in the team achieving goals and objectives beyond the sum of the parts of the team. I refer to this type of group as a "transcendent team."

A transcendent team goes beyond the daily delivery of tasks and reaches a level of performance that goes beyond the expected delivery. They transcend normal team behaviors. What do I mean by transcendent?

As an example, from history (1958) of what a transcendent team achieved, consider the scenario that led to developing a Cannonball Adderley album, which became one of the top jazz albums in history. A group of musicians met at the Van Gelder Studio in Hackensack, New Jersey. Rudy Van Gelder established the studio in his parents' house while he still attended high school. Because of the limitations of his studio, he innovated the way he placed the microphones in the small space. He altered the sounds of individual instruments and produced a sound unlike any other at the time. The sound became known as his "Blue Note" sound, which has a greater sense of volume. Julian "Cannonball" Adderley led the group that day. Other musicians in the room that day included Miles Davis on trumpet, Hank Jones on piano, Sam Jones on bass, and Art Blakey on drums, who were accomplished musicians.

Listening to this music, you can hear each contributor adds to something bigger than the individual music and adds to the whole sound. There was a lot of individual talent in the room; but, together, they created something bigger than their individual talent. They "transcended" their separate talents to create something that was truly magical and beyond the sum of the parts. It really was "something else." This is an example of a transcendent team, as their achievement went beyond original expectations. Together, they delivered above-average performance to create exceptional music.

Many people have been part of a team that goes beyond the daily delivery of tasks and reaches a level of performance that goes beyond the expected delivery. These teams are special, and there is a feeling that they transcend the normal team behaviors. They are "transcendent" teams. The role of an energetic, impactful leader is to lead teams so they can be transcendent in this way.

As a leader, you also may be involved in a collaboration with other groups or teams that are outside your direct control. These collaborations may involve alliances or partnerships with other companies or organizations. Chapter 10 provides insights and advice on effective leadership in collaborations.

My own experience highlights characteristics of transcendent project teams that are common in the drug-development process. Individuals from all disciplines involved in the drug-development process comprise these teams. They are involved in solving complex problems and may work together for many years. The team leader is accountable for delivering the drug to market with his team. Individual project team members are also accountable for their piece of the process.

There is no doubt that in a lot of cases they feel mutually accountable for delivering the drug. In other cases, they only feel accountable for their piece of the work. This often reflects in the way companies reward and recognize them. Often, the line manager (from an individual's discipline) determines an individual's pay rise, promotion, and bonuses, rather than the project team leader. There may be input to the line manager from the team, but the power of reward does not lie with the team. One reason for this is that a project team member may sit on multiple teams.

I am not arguing that this type of team cannot be successful. But unless there is mutual accountability within the team (including reward and recognition for team member performance), it becomes more difficult to form a transcendent team.

What characteristics do transcendent teams share? In my experience, they have a level of trust for each other, enabling them to know that each member will deliver without having to ask and each member will go the extra mile for the team. They have a shared consciousness and understanding of the mission of the team. They share a mutual accountability around a mission they regard as being important and meaningful. They know each other's strengths and complement each other to overcome their weaknesses.

In addition, there seems to be an interconnectivity within a transcendent team so that not everything must come through one leader; everyone is willing to step up as leaders in different situations. They have a strong social bond and chemistry and get along with each other, at least while involved in the task at hand. And, obviously, each team member brings a high level of talent. Bottom line: Their way of working with each other results in operational excellence.

How can you create teams that successfully deliver your strategic goals and vision? In my experience, there are four factors that energizing, impactful leaders should consider in building transcendent teams: setting clear purpose and goals in the context; team formation; team charter; and team development and decision-making.

Setting Clear Purpose and Goals in Context

Energizing, impactful leaders have clear purpose and powerful strategic goals that focus their energy and inspire others in the team to follow. When leading a team that you want to shape into becoming a transcendent team, you must clearly communicate a vision and purpose that the team believes in and will secure their commitment. You need to take this a step further and ensure you develop a purpose specific to the team, which also shows the team that achieving the desired strategic goal is doable for them.

Creating a team purpose leverages their emotions, which not only helps get their commitment but also motivates input from the team to drive more energy in achieving the strategic goal. A critical point about developing a team purpose statement and performance goals is that it should align with the larger mission of the wider organization. In my experience, it demotivates a team when there is no clear connection with the goals of the overall company or enterprise.

The purpose of the team helps to define a mission aligned with the wider organization and is a purpose that is developed and owned by the team. It forms the basis of the team's "shared consciousness." Shared consciousness is one of the intangible aspects of a transcendent team. It is what it means to be part of the team means. It is shared understanding within the team of what the team is about and why it exists. This shared consciousness may only be understood fully by the team members and sets them apart from the rest of the organization.

Some of the most successful teams I see have a passion for their team and their team purpose that gives them a greater connection and allegiance to their team than to the wider organization. The team is in some ways set apart from the rest of the organization and is sometimes viewed as a group of renegades. This can sometimes cause some friction with the team members and cause them to feel torn between the team and their other functions. If you, as the leader, properly manage this tension, it will not stifle creativity and innovation. If managed badly, such tension can lead to conflict and wasting energy and time fighting non-productive turf wars.

In my experience, it is demotivating to the team when there is no clear connection with the purpose of the overall company or enterprise. For example, when I worked in R&D, I wanted to see that the purpose for the team directly aligned to the goals of R&D. The main reason for this is that if the team was not aligned with the wider organization, there was a risk that their activities would be viewed as low priority and might be starved of resources the team needed to be successful.

Teams are not islands unto themselves. They survive by understanding the surrounding seas. As their leader, you need competency in system thinking so that you can help your team think through how their team fits in with their system.

A good example of this is that most large pharmaceutical companies operate on a "matrix structure" with functional lines on one axis and project teams on the other. From the project team's perspective, they are part of a complex system in this matrix structure. This type of team needs to be clear about how the matrix system works if they are to be successful. They need to have a clear understanding of the stakeholders for the project within the system and work to keep these stakeholders aligned with the aims of the project and obtaining and keeping their support. In fact, I would argue that one of most important skills of a project leader and team members in this type of project is to understand the context in which the team operates and to ensure support and alignment of key stakeholders.

Leaders should establish clear performance goals with a transcendent team. These goals form the basis for which the team has mutual accountability. Team goals should be viewed as urgent in nature. The team needs clarity about why the objectives need to be achieved now. Again, if the team goals are not viewed as urgent and critical, there is a risk that they will be seen as low priority. The team must see goals as meaningful and achievable. They must be challenging to a point of motivating the team to succeed beyond their normal performance but not so challenging that they are viewed as impossible.

Keep in mind that a transcendent team differs from other work groups in that team members have mutual accountability around goals. Like the team's purpose, team goals should align with the overall system of which the team is a part.

Team Formation

Energizing, impactful leaders know how to form effective teams. The initial formation stages are important and should be intentionally managed. When forming a team a few questions should be considered. What is the ideal size of the team? Who should be part of the team? What are the crucial first steps?

In my experience, the ideal size of a team is between ten to fifteen people. With anything less than ten, you run the risk of not having diverse experiences and ideas. With more than fifteen, the group becomes more difficult to manage, particularly ensuring that everyone is included in the discussion and that their voices are heard.

Often, the challenge is how to get all the necessary skills and representation on a team without it becoming difficult to manage. For some complex team projects, bigger teams are needed; these larger numbers can be accommodated by forming sub-teams. Bear in mind that as the team develops you may need to bring new members onto the team or replace team members who leave the organization.

You should appoint or recruit team members based on their skills and the value they bring to the table. Members of cross-functional teams should also be selected as representatives of other groups. For example, in a team that is formed to develop a new drug, there is a need to have representation on the team of the functional units involved in the drug-development process.

Transcendent teams are diverse, but they also take full advantage of the different views, experiences, and perspectives that they bring to the table. As a leader of a successful transcendent team, you need smart, engaged, motivated, people around you who can thrive, have clear purpose, cooperate with others, and have a high degree of emotional intelligence. Transcendent teams recognize the strengths of team members and make sure they have a good balance of strengths that complement each other.

The first crucial step in forming a team is to have a kickoff meeting. This ideally should be a face-to-face meeting, but that is not always possible. There are three objectives of that meeting: first, to agree the purpose and goals as described above; second, to get to know each other; and finally, to agree on how team members will work together. This final point will involve agreeing to a team charter, and this will be discussed in greater detail later in this chapter.

The kickoff meeting is the start of a team getting to know each other. Transcendent teams make the effort to work to understand each other's strengths and weaknesses and complement each other to build on their strengths and overcome their weaknesses. To do this, they need to do more than work together on specific tasks; they also need to spend time building relationships and learning about each other from a social perspective. If the team has the opportunity to meet face to face at the workplace, then a social gathering should be included. If the team is a virtual group, they need to set aside some time to interact virtually as a social group.

The efforts to help team members understand each other's strengths, weaknesses, and work styles should occur at the formation stage of a team. Many tools are available for this purpose such as the widely known Myers-Briggs Type Indicator ® for assessing behavior and personality traits and the Hogan Personality Inventory (HPI). Some companies follow up these assessment results by sharing team members' profiles during a facilitated session and a team discussion about styles and how best the team can work together.

As team members become aware of their respective styles, strengths, and weaknesses, they understand how to adjust the way they work together. Getting to know each other also helps to build trust and form a bond within the team.

For larger teams, I find it beneficial to have a dedicated facilitator whose primary role on the team is to monitor and manage the team's dynamics. The facilitator may help you as the leader and the team to be more effective in forming the team.

Another outcome of teams getting to know each other is that team members can appreciate how each other will react to different situations. Team members need to be sensitive to other team members' feelings and emotions. Transcendent teams have a high degree of intuitively understanding the dynamics within the team.

If you study any team, you will notice that each team member has a preferred role they like to play on the team. These preferred roles represent a strength that an individual has for the team. A well-balanced team has members who are willing to take on these roles to balance how the team make up and complement each other. For instance, some people are better at coordinating while others are better at implementing.

You may want to demonstrate to the team what happens with the differences in roles. One example I see used effectively is to bring the team together for a task such as building a tower out of materials in the room. I observed this in a large workshop, so they split the group into teams of eight people. Each team's task was building a tower out of materials in the room such as paper, scissors, paper clips, tape, and general office supplies. The team that built the highest tower within a set period (forty-five minutes or an hour) would win a small prize.

They then split each team of eight into two groups. Two people would observe the team activity and could not help in building the tower; their role was to make notes of who did what. The other six people were instructed to design and build the tower. At the end of the activity, the organization measured the towers and declared a winning team. The observers then described what happened in each team.

In my experience observing several of these exercises, I see several things happening. Some teams jump straight into building towers, which often collapse. They then try again. Other teams spend some time designing and planning the perfect tower but run out of time to build the tower. The important part of the exercise is the debrief at the end. Each person on the team exhibits their preferred team role style.

These initial stages of building a team should focus on building trust. Transcendent teams have a high degree of trust and intentionally build relationships through their communication and actions and by being authentic with each other. Each team member should understand his or her authentic self and act in a way that is consistent with that individual's values. Authenticity also requires that team members be courageous enough to feel comfortable disclosing their true selves and showing vulnerability.

Team Conversation

An important tool that is used by transcendent teams is the team charter. The team charter can be viewed as a contract between team members. Your role as a leader is to drive the process of creating this document and to get commitment and agreement with the team members. In my experience, the best team charters include the overall purpose for the team, function of the team, team objectives, and assumptions about the system. This final point includes how the team's work will fit into other groups activities and the interconnections with other teams.

Another important component of the charter is ground rules. These are agreements on how the team will work and behave with each other. A good example of what may be part of the ground rules is how the team will make decisions. Decision-making should involve the team including diverse views and ideas. This takes work, but the cost of excluding people on the team is high. Transcendent teams avoid people feeling there are in-groups and out-groups. In other words, everyone is involved in the strategy and decisions a team makes.

I am not suggesting that everyone must agree with decisions made by the team, but they should feel that their voice is heard and that they are included. Inclusion, in this sense, is an issue for everyone on the team; it means having an environment that includes all viewpoints. I would suggest that one of the most important tasks of a team leader is to find ways to ensure everyone is included and ensure no team member feels excluded.

The team can also agree on how they will communicate and commit to listen to each other. Transcendent team members intentionally listen to each other and develop active and empathetic listening. They manage their contributions to discussions (verbal and written) and value quality over quantity. By listening effectively, they show that they are open to the input and ideas from others and can learn from diverse sources.

The team also can agree to have an open mindset and be willing to learn from their successes and failures. The team can then adjust their strategies based on what they learn. It is especially important that a team in a fast, dynamic, changing environment be open to growth, challenging themselves, and their desire to learn.

The team ground rules can also include a commitment from the team members to be present for the team and not distracted during team discussions. This involves having the team members show undivided attention during team interactions. As a team leader, one of your roles is to protect the team from distractions, including those generated from your own actions. You also need to protect the team from interruptions and let them get on with their jobs.

Successfully delivering the desired strategic outcome depends significantly on your reducing the team's worries about failure and being judged. Frame failures as opportunities to learn how to do things differently. If the team worries about failure and their consequences, they will do what is safe and not what is creative.

Team ground rules can also outline how conflict in the team will be resolved. As a team leader, you should be clear that you regard conflict as thinking and conflict can be raised safely. It is important that the team does not suppress conflict. Often, what is not said is important. The worst possible scenario is that a team member has a view or a piece of information critical to the team activities but is afraid to raise it because he or she does not want to be in conflict or cause disharmony in the team. In a transcendent team, the members understand that it is important to raise conflict, and they do not avoid conflict. Once raised, the team can resolve conflicting views.

Managing conflict is also an important skill for transcendent teams. I recommend that teams determine effective ways to deal with conflict and include this information in their team charter.

If the team meets virtually, they also should establish ground rules for working in this environment. This would include how they use technologies. Care should be taken that all team members have access to the necessary technology and ability to connect with each other. It is also worth assessing the level of competence for each team member in using the necessary technology.

As the team forms, it is valuable for the team to discuss how they will work effectively, develop build ground rules, and commit to intentionally behaving in this way. Ground rules may evolve; and in my experience, it is worth revisiting them regularly to remind the team of their commitments.

Team Development

Typically, team members express different feelings at different stages in team development. Some may wonder why the team was formed and what it will do. They may ask themselves if the team is important and whether they need to prioritize time for this team. They wonder if the team will be successful or a waste of time. They may think, "I am already busy with my day job and do not need another team."

Others may have concerns about what the team expects from them. If they do not already know the other team members, they may be suspicious of others' motives and agendas. They wonder if the team will get along or be in conflict all the time. They may think, "Will this team be a positive experience or just a pain in the neck?"

Feelings of being anxious and suspicious are not uncommon at the start of a new team. Team members have a lot of questions and a high level of uncertainty. Part of your role as the leader at this stage is to be aware of their feelings and work to reduce uncertainty and provide clarity and direction about the team.

When a team forms, the team members are often polite with each other at first, not knowing how people act. Other team members may stand off or be reserved, staying quiet until they see how the team shapes up. Both you, as the leader, and each team member needs a high degree of empathy to recognize the feelings others experience.

With a good team charter, as described above, there may be less uncertainty about what the team needs to try to achieve and how it will go about that mission. This is important because, at the outset, some individuals may not be fully on board with the team.

For example, if an organization forms a team to lead a major organizational change, some team members may fear that this change will impact their status quo. They may realize that a change is good or necessary for the organization, but they perceive a negative impact on them personally. This may cause them to resist the rest of the team in the early stages. They retain their individual objectives and agenda and are not yet aligned or bonded with the team.

Others at the outset may have a feeling of doubt that this team activity is worth doing, especially if it disrupts their status quo. They may express these concerns in the early stages, and this can lead to conflict. Arguments and what appears to be fighting between team members may break out.

It is important for the team to get these conflicts out on the table so that they can manage them, and the team can work through solutions. If conflicts are not raised and resolved, there is a real danger that the team will get stuck in this phase of development. The role of a leader in this stage is to have a high degree of empathy to recognize the feelings others may experience and express. Once these wary team members start to feel part of the team and feel a higher level of trust with the leader and other team members, they will start to accept that the other team members' intentions are true. Those who expressed resistance, reservation, or skepticism will be less inclined to continue reacting in that way.

The team's early successes will help enhance the team's positive feelings and energy. In contrast, my experience is that a team may go back to the earlier conflict-ridden environment if the team experiences significant challenges or setbacks instead of early good outcomes. I recommend that you and your team address these feelings head on and manage conflicts that occur.

In transcendent teams, their effectiveness and trust grow, and they spend time working together. Over time, they build ways of communicating that enable flexibility in their approaches to their project. Following their early quick wins, they become more confident about their ability to solve bigger problems and tasks and about achieving their final objectives. They feel good about being part of the team, and they perform effectively.

Recall that I stated earlier that transcendent teams achieve outcomes that go beyond expectations. To achieve this state, team members go beyond their expected roles, taking on new roles that will help the team, even if the team needs something from them that is not in their best interest. Their willingness to do so stems from their having an open mindset.

Transcendent teams have a high degree of intuitively understanding the dynamics within the team. As the leader, you will help them test the closed mindset of their assumptions and develop an open mindset.

Team Decision-Making

Understanding and managing team decision-making is another important skill required for building a transcendent team. Why? Because the decisions teams make will determine their actions.

As mentioned above, decision making is a key process for a transcendent team. Effective leaders have an ability to make decisions (either alone or with a group) regarding actions that lead to success. Decisions may be big decisions (such as a big financial investment), or small decisions made many times a day (such as how to work with someone). Great leaders have a robust decision-making process. However, in a team setting, everyone in the team (not just the leader) makes decisions, and this is especially true in transcendent teams.

Transcendent teams' decision-making process considers the following questions. "Do we have to make the decision now, or is it better to wait for more data or a better understanding of the situation?" They seek to balance both the short-term and long-term impact of actions. They also ask, "What are our assumptions for each option we intend to consider?" This helps the team determine its level of confidence for each option.

For example, when considering the best course of action to develop a drug, there may be three options: (1) Perform a small study with a few patients to gather safety data; (2) perform a larger study with more study parameters in a selected number of patients to gather safety data but also start to understand if the drug has the desired effect; or (3) perform a large study with many patients to assess if the drug works in a broader population of patients.

Defining all pros and cons of each option so that an informed decision can be made requires a rigorous decision-making process. This process also identifies any assumptions in place.

For example, the benefits of the first option are that the drug company can obtain data quickly. The risk is that the option could slow down the overall project plan. The benefits of the second scenario are that the team can obtain more data, but the process would take longer and would be more expensive. The benefits of the third option are that the project will reach a broader endpoint more quickly. The risks are that this major financial investment could result in negative outcomes and prove to be a waste of time and money. There is an assumption for the third option that there is enough positive data obtained so far that the risk is worth taking. There may be more confidence that a small study would be successful whereas a larger study may not.

Like effective leaders, transcendent teams are aware of emotions and biases that can influence their decisions; so, they try to minimize their negative impacts and, instead, use their emotions in a positive way. Their decision-making process enables them to make decisions with all team members aligned with the overall goals of the team.

Consider the behavior of teenagers as an example of these concepts. Teens can be headstrong and have strong opinions. Parents are concerned that their teens will make bad decisions when they are out with their friends and the parents do not have a direct influence. In most cases, these fears are not grounded in experience but, rather, in doubt.

Parents hope their teens listened to lessons over the years and have a framework for making decisions that will not get them into trouble. Parental influence over a teenager is less impactful than peer influence. If teens have a decision-making process driven solely by their emotions and not involving an analytical assessment of the potential consequences of their decisions, they may get into trouble. If they have a value system that balances emotions with a core set of principles, they are less likely to make decisions they will regret.

The same is true for teams. You may not realize this, but teams also need guidelines for team members making decisions outside the team environment.

In team projects, a high degree of collaboration often needs to occur to come to a decision. There are times that decisions should be made at the top in the command-and-control style. For instance, if a child runs into a street of fast-moving traffic, there needs to be a direct command to get out of the street. In team decisions in the workplace, it could be that an option is not clear, and the team needs to work together to define the options for a decision. Most of the time, teams do not use a command-and-control decision-making style. Optimally, they make decisions through consensus with all parties having an equal responsibility for the decisions. Team members may not necessarily agree with the decision, but they must support the decision.

Energizing, impactful leaders and transcendent teams also use the technique of using pilot studies before they make a decision. They may split a big decision into smaller ones. They pilot an approach, gather data on the impact of the decision, and adjust their approach. They learn from pilot studies and use the learnings to ensure flexibility in their approach to decision-making.

Effective teams and leaders know that team decision-making is a process, not an event. They prepare for a decision by gathering data, defining options, performing a risk-versus-benefit analysis, and gathering views and opinions. This information helps them agree on which option and course of action to follow. They have the courage of their convictions. They commit to a decision and follow through on the actions even if the decision may not be popular or challenging.

After they implement their decisions and take action, they measure success and determine whether they need to modify actions. Transcendent teams manage all pieces of the decision-making process, and they often document their process into their team charter.

Another recommendation is for the team leader to make sure the team focuses on the priorities for the team, those activities and tasks that will deliver the team's purpose and strategic goals. This is especially important when team conflicts arise purely from personality clashes. The team should always work to resolve conflict that focuses on the work, not on individual feelings. When team members get to know each other at the outset of team formation and seek to understand each other's point of view, this empathy can help understanding individual motives in a conflict.

ENERGIZE TO IMPACT

Energizing, Impactful Leadership in Action: Building a Transcendent Team

Naomi sat in her office and took a deep breath. It seemed like this was the first time she was able to stop and think for the past two weeks. Things were crazy, even for her standards.

Her thoughts were interrupted by a knock at the door. One of the maintenance staff wanted to put a new sign on her door and asked if it was a good time. The sign displayed her name and the title "Chief Executive Officer." Her initial irritation at being interrupted was replaced by an almost surreal feeling that this sign was about her. She worked hard at the medical device company. It was small when she joined but enjoyed incredible growth in the past ten years due to several successful launches of new products.

The growing company was different now. It was a strong mid-sized company with offices in the United States, Europe, China, and Japan. Her hard work over the years paid off with roles in the company with increasing responsibility. She loved the work and the company, and she felt its products had a big impact on patients and improving their quality of life.

Less than a month ago, her boss announced he would leave the company and she was appointed as the new CEO. Naomi knew this job would not be easy. New regulations in the medical device field and changes in the marketplace lowered the barrier of entry for other companies to compete in their market space. This was one of the main reasons that her boss decided to retire. Becoming CEO was the start of a new and exciting journey for Naomi.

Naomi had a reputation of being a driven and highly successful individual contributor. Others recognized that she was a good team player and knew that her success was equally being part of a team as well as an individual. She learned early in her career that her individual efforts would not be enough. Groups of scientists from multiple disciplines work together in making a scientific breakthrough successful. There were some talented scientists in her company who generated some great ideas for new devices that could change people's lives. Her challenge, as an energizing, impactful leader, was to harness these ideas and ensure that the right people formed the right team to develop and deliver the medical devices to patients and the market.

Naomi realized that her company's success would require that she form and lead a highly effective leadership team. The former CEO built a particularly good team of which she was a part before taking on the CEO role; however, she had some challenges with this team. Several team members thought they deserved the CEO role. She had to manage this situation carefully, as she knew that there was a risk that some people might leave because they did not get the top job. She also realized that continuing company growth meant her leadership team would need to go beyond their current performance. The key question on Naomi's mind as she took on the new role? How could she create and lead a team that goes beyond the sum of the parts and perform at a higher level? In other words, how could she create and manage a transcendent team?

She realized that for the company to succeed she would need to form and lead a highly effective group of leaders who were leading R&D and commercial operations around the world. This group had accountability for their individual functions, but Naomi felt that a key next step was for these leaders to come together as a team and share a mutual accountability for the success of the company. This mutual accountability would be reflected in the goals and objectives that each member of her new leadership team would have. It would also be reflected in the performance bonuses, reward, and recognition the team would receive.

The important concept that Naomi introduced was that no individual or function could be viewed as successful unless the whole team were successful. She felt strongly that the members of her team should support each other. In the past, there was some "silo behavior." Members of the previous group would battle hard for their budget and resources for their silo, and the stronger functions won these battles at the cost of some other groups' needs. Naomi felt that there should not be winners and losers; they should all win, or all lose.

Her team would oversee the running of the business and collectively decide where to invest. For example, if a new project came from R&D, they would collectively commit to bring the product to market and commercialize it. If a major investment were needed to open a new site or market, they would collectively commit to that investment. She wanted the team to work with long-term strategic goals in mind. This team needed to be sustainable and in place for the long haul.

Naomi was clear in her vision for how she wanted to run the business. She wanted a cooperative, mutually accountable team that would share with her the responsibility of running the business, setting vision and strategy for the company, and collectively make major investment decisions. She knew that, as CEO, that ultimate responsibility was hers; but she knew that the company would have a bigger impact if everyone were energized to succeed.

The first meeting of her leadership team occurred about three weeks after she became CEO. In these early days, she knew that the team had to formulate a strategic plan that would engage and motivate her organization. In the first meeting, she challenged the team to think strategically and define a purpose, mission, and strategy that would excite them to go beyond the amazing growth the company achieved in the past few years. She hired a team coach to help facilitate this discussion.

They started from a clear understanding of their current strengths and performed an analysis that helped them to define the market they wanted to pursue. They identified their strengths and vulnerabilities and their opportunities to grow. They also performed an analysis of the threat to their current market position. They spent many hours agreeing on their purpose and why the organization should exist. Naomi felt confident that everyone on the team was committed to this strategy and, if they were successful, they could have a major impact on patients' lives and see the company grow.

The next step for the team was to perform a system analysis answering the question of how this team fit in with the systems of which they were a part. When the team looked at the internal organization, it was clear that their role as a team was to lead the company. They were also responsible for creating a culture that attracted the best talent and partners and motivating and engaging the employees.

Naomi hired a team coach to help her keep developing her team. The first thing the coach suggested is that the team needed to get to know each other and build trust among the team members. From Naomi's perspective, this first face-to-face workshop was a great success. They increased the level of team awareness, team empathy, and an open mindset. The team's feedback was also very good. Previously, they had no chance to get to know each other well, but now they had a real appreciation of each other's strengths, weaknesses, emotions, and feelings.

There were three outcomes from the meeting. First, the team agreed on ground rules governing how they would work together and make the most of everyone's unique contribution. Second, the level of trust increased, not only between individual team members but across the team. Third, they all agreed that they would meet face to face at least three times a year and include team building as part of their regular meeting agendas. Having a team coach working with them gave them a resource that could give regular feedback to how the team was working, so they agreed coaching would be part of all their team meetings.

As Naomi's leadership team started working together, they moved through the early stages of development and started becoming productive. Their ground rules included an agreement to intentionally create positive energy in the team and act for the good of the team. These ground rules aimed at having consensus around team behavior including communication and listening to each other; authenticity; acting with self-confidence, passion, and enthusiasm; and being present.

They committed to creating a positive team environment that included giving each other immediate feedback. They agreed to view failure as an opportunity to learn and learned from their successes. Naomi worked hard to protect the team from many distractions and kept them focused on the tasks at hand. She gave the team clear priorities around tasks that would deliver on their purpose and strategic goals. She also formed a diverse team, and the team committed to include everyone, listen carefully to every point of view, and work hard to find common ground. Although they did most of their communicating virtually, they decided to meet face to face on occasions.

They included the ground rules in their team charter, and the team coach was very valuable in helping the team live up to their ground rules by giving the team regular feedback and performing a meeting review at the end of each meeting.

Naomi was happy with the way she formed her leadership team with the right people on the team sharing a vision of what they tried to achieve with the company. The team overcame some challenges in the first few months. The team also identified how they would manage their team dynamics and be sensitive to the emotions and feelings of all team members.

CHARLES S. DORMER

Chapter Summary

One key way that energizing, impactful leaders deliver their strategy and results is by forming and leading transcendent teams. These teams go beyond the sum of their parts and achieve outcomes above expectations. Leaders set a clear purpose and goals for the team in the context of their system and wider organization. They intentionally manage team formation, recruiting team members with complementary strengths and influence on stakeholders. They give team members time to get to know each other's strengths, opportunities for, and preferred team role styles.

They work with the team and have conversations that include purpose, objectives, and an agreed way to work with each other (ground rules). This results in a team charter. They manage the development of the team and define decision-making processes.

The aim of a transcendent team is not just to form an effective team but also to deliver actions and activities that are meaningful to strategic goals.

Key Learnings for Leading Transcendent Teams

- Energizing, impactful leaders build transcendent teams by managing styles, roles, and team dynamics.
- They pull together the right team composed of complementary skills, who commit to a common purpose, sense of urgency, performance goals, and approach.
- They form and manage effective teams that are diverse and take advantage of that diversity.
- They identify different styles and recognize that all are important for an effective team. They make the most of the different styles.
- They develop teams through all phases, beginning with formation through developing high performance and delivering the desired goal. They are aware of which phase the team is in and facilitate the team getting to the next phase or level.

- They understand the challenges when teams are virtual. They leverage virtual distances and avoid pitfalls that inhibit performance due to virtual team dynamics.

Action Plan for Becoming Effective in Leading Transcendent Teams

In your action plan, take time to reflect on your strengths and your opportunity for growth. This self-reflection has two parts. First, review the following questions and rate yourself for a strength or an opportunity for growth for each question. Next, think about actions that you can take to enhance your strength or develop your opportunity for growth.

1. Are you effective at putting together the right team including diversity and inclusion?
2. Do you develop mutual accountability in a team for team objectives and goals?
3. Do you analyze internal and external systems that impact the team?
4. Are you effective in fostering team awareness and team members knowing each other's strengths, weaknesses, and preferred work styles?
5. Are you effective at fostering team empathy, encouraging the team to understand their emotions and feelings and those of others on the team?
6. How well do you understand team dynamics? Can you move the team to high performance levels?
7. How well do you encourage a team open mindset? Do you encourage the team to overcome closed mindsets and learn as a team?
8. Do you foster positive team presence by encouraging effective communication and listening?
9. Do you foster a positive virtual team environment and minimize impact of people being physically apart?
10. Do you effectively use team member strengths in terms of team roles?

Chapter 10
Optimizing Collaborations

"In the long history of humankind (and animal kind, too) those who learned to collaborate and improvise most effectively have prevailed."

Charles Darwin

In addition to working with transcendent teams, as described in Chapter 9, energizing, impactful leaders work with other types of groups that are involved in delivering results. These groups are alliances, partnerships, or collaborations involving people in different companies or organizations. An important factor in leading these types of groups is that these entities are not under the leader's direct control. For ease in discussing how to lead these types of relationships, I refer to all these various types of relationships as "alliances."

Alliances come in many forms and range from a relatively simple collaboration between two companies to access novel ideas or market a product, or more complex collaborations involving many parties. Alliances include simple partnerships where one organization accesses an innovative technology developed by a second company or academic organization. Alliances also include relationships that involve licensing from an entity of equity outside of the strategic interest of the company.

Finally, alliances can be collaborations between a company, academic, or commercial organization to discover, develop, or market innovative ideas or technologies. The objective of this type of collaboration is to discover innovative targets/technologies, to share intellectual property (IP), and for each party to share rewards from developing the IP.

When more than two parties work together in this way, they form co-creative, de-centralized, complex networks. In my experience, successful leadership requires being effective in creating and leading these co-creative, decentralized, complex networks. The networks involve groups of people who have the competencies or intellectual property that is needed to deliver the goals. By creating an alliance, they lower transaction costs and make it easier to do business across boundaries.

This characteristic is particularly true in science and technology. People used to think of this field as a "genius"-based endeavor; now groups of scientists work together in making a breakthrough from many different laboratories. Besides the fields of science and technology, it is also true in other endeavors that require partnerships and alliances to create a supply chain, sales, or marketing organizations.

A good example of the leadership challenge in such alliances is research and development in the pharmaceutical industry. Pharmaceutical research companies realize that no one company can have access to all innovation. This led to the need to form strategic alliances with other companies and organizations. To ensure access to innovation, novel drug targets, and technologies, large pharmaceutical discovery research organizations must leverage internal and external collaborative relationships ("collaborations").

This need led to many deals among large pharmaceutical companies, academic organizations, and biotechnology companies. These deals include a significant investment on all sides. This industry increasingly relies on licensing deals with biotechnology companies and collaborations with academic organizations to provide innovative drugs. Creating such relationships led to a decreased internal capability in several companies and a reliance on co-creation of innovative science in collaboration with several partners.

These situations led to the need for leaders to change their behavior from using authoritarian power in hierarchical structures to, instead, influencing others in de-centralized matrices.

An essential core competence for any alliance is the ability to identify appropriate partners, collaborate with other organizations, and manage the interface with those partners to reach strategic goals and take advantage of unexpected synergies. Companies or organizations must develop and maintain core competencies that make them attractive as alliance partners. The challenges of each alliance are different, complex, and require leaders with the ability to exercise a high degree of collaborative behaviors and skills.

Challenges of Co-creative, De-centralized, Complex Alliances

From a leadership perspective, there are several challenges associated with leading complex alliances. In forming a collaborative alliance between two or more organizations, leaders need to create an environment that builds trust and allows parties to share ideas and information freely. This is essential if the expectation is that the alliance will lead to innovative ideas. In my experience, challenges to building this collaborative environment include the size and culture of the alliance partners, speed in decision-making, organizational political systems, legal complexities, and differing motivations and agendas.

Challenge of Size and Culture of Alliance Partners

Most collaborative alliances are between organizations of different sizes and with different cultures. A large company is very different from a small, start-up company; and both are very different from an academic or government institution. An alliance may represent a small part of a large company's operation. But in a small company, the work of an alliance may be the primary or only priority. Although important, the alliance may not be a high priority for the larger company, and it may be difficult to get management attention or resources assigned to the alliance.

The culture of these different-sized organizations is unique and can be extremely different. For example, a large company may be hierarchical or very political in the way it makes decisions. An academic organization may be very bureaucratic in nature and require a lot of committees and paperwork. In contrast, a small, start-up company may be nimble and agile, making decisions quickly. These examples of culture may not apply just because of the organizations' size.

Cultural differences can be a barrier to success if they lead to miscommunication, misunderstanding, and misinterpreting messages. This can lead to suspicion of intention and mistrust. These issues magnify significantly when three or more parties collaborate.

In addition, there is increased complexity associated with collaborations involving organizations from different regions in the world. There may be language differences to overcome or elements associated with national cultures. Also, there is the added challenge of time differences due to different locations. Face-to-face meetings may be difficult to arrange on a regular basis, and these meetings are particularly important in the early stages of an alliance. Strategic leaders involved in alliances should invest time in getting to know the culture and nature of the partner organizations.

Challenge of Speed of Decision-Making

The second challenge to creating a collaborative environment is the relative speed of decision-making within the partners. Typically, large companies can mobilize resources on a global scale but tend to be slow and unadaptable or inflexible in decision-making. With scale comes complexity and bureaucracy. Smaller companies are nimble, and their decision-making process is less complex. They also can make decisions more quickly because they are limited in scope and scale. Academic organizations and government organizations bring their own bureaucracies and may be perceived as slow.

Differences in decision-making also may be due to the degree of empowerment of individuals involved in the alliance. Organizations with centralization of power and/or hierarchical structures with un-empowered employees tend to be slower decision-makers because decisions must involve several layers of management. In a collaborative alliance, slow decision-making can stifle innovation, leading to slowing of projects and suspicion of bad intentions.

Challenge of Organizational Political Systems

Another potential barrier to an innovative collaborative environment for an alliance relates to the collaborators' internal political systems. Each party has "fiefdoms" and patronages that they need to manage. The political systems differ greatly based on the type of organizations involved in the alliance.

Effective management of these politics will have an impact on decision-making speed and on ensuring the necessary resources are available to support the alliance and ensure all parties view projects as high priority. There is a potential for disconnect here, particularly if a large company has many conflicting priorities and the alliance is one of only a few priorities for a start-up company. Again, the impact of misalignment of priorities could be that it starves the collaboration of necessary resources and skills.

Moreover, issues can arise if the parties perceive decisions are made through subversive or overt political maneuvering. This could include escalation of issues in the alliance prematurely to senior management or bypassing layers of management. Inappropriate political maneuvering within an alliance will quickly lead to lack of trust and conflict.

Challenge of Legal Complexities

Creating and protecting intellectual property is a key driver in an innovation-driven alliance. Legal agreements are more complicated when multiple parties are involved in alliances. Sharing of risk and reward is a key driver for establishing alliances from the perspective of a large company, a start-up, or an academic organization. For an alliance to be collaborative, leaders must create a legal environment that is clear, well defined and understood by all participants involved in the alliance. If this is not the case, the legal framework can suppress the participants from sharing information and ideas. This clearly will result in stifling innovation in the alliance.

Challenge of Differing Motivations and Agendas

Another challenge that a collaborative alliance faces is the resolution of the differing agendas and motivations of the collaboration partners. Each party entering an alliance has a motivation for entering the relationship. The motivation may be to access resources or skills that are complimentary to their own skills. Or it may be to access innovative ideas or IP to add to their own position in a particular field.

For instance, in a large company, the motivation may be to access a competence that is not developed within the company. Motivation for a small, start-up company may be to access an alternative source of funding or to share risk in developing a technology.

Parties often resolve conflicting motivations when negotiating the deal before committing to a collaboration. However, often they do not fully resolve differing motivations, which can lead to disillusionment and mistrust in the collaboration.

In addition, each party may bring a different agenda to the table, particularly in respect to how the collaboration should work. Mistrust can develop if parties believe one agenda wins at the cost of the other. This belief can result in one party feeling exploited; so, the feeling needs to be managed effectively. Each party can become disillusioned if the collaboration does not meet their expectations.

These issues of different motivations, agendas, and expectations can magnify if multiple partners are involved. An example is the issue of creating alliance termination strategies. Alliances should define a clear exit strategy based on a time milestone or based on a clear deliverable. As the collaboration progresses, there may be different views on when partners want to end the alliance. This is less of a problem if the parties perceive the alliance as successful. It is a much larger issue if the collaboration does not deliver the expected results.

Innovation is not always a predictable activity and does not always go according to plan. Under the above conditions, some parties may want to cut their losses and withdraw while others may want to give the collaboration more time and/or resources to try again. These are difficult decisions to make and manage.

As described above, clearly there can be some significant barriers to successfully managing a complex alliance. This impact can be detrimental if the expectation of the alliance is to access innovative ideas in a collaborative partnership. Strategic leaders involved in these alliances should invest time to understand these potential barriers and understand the alliance system.

Alliance Leadership in Practice

Energizing, impactful leaders involved in complex collaborations must keep in mind both delivering their strategy and goals and creating energy through their leadership. In my research of critical factors in alliances, I identified those that relate to the "task and delivery" and elements that concern the "trust and relationship."

Obviously, both sets of factors are important and essential for a successful alliance to reach expected goals and take advantage of unexpected synergies. So, let us further explore these critical factors and how energizing, impactful leaders use them to drive for results.

Task and Delivery Factors

The task-related elements include reasons for entering an alliance; identifying the right partner; identifying potential synergies between the collaborators; driving to outcomes and deliverables; and putting in place a structure for planning, governance, and decision-making.

When dealing with outside partners, there is a greater need to be an energizing, impactful leader who can create energy in others through relationship and trust-based elements. These elements include organization cultures, chemistry between partners, working together to collaborate, alliance leadership, communication, and building trust.

Reasons for Entering an Alliance

Just as leaders need to determine a purpose and clear, well-defined strategic goals, the same principles apply to alliances. Each party has a reason for joining the partnership. The alliance also must have clear strategy and purpose that comes from a convergence of interests of all parties. In other words, all parties involved in the alliance need to be clear as to why they are in the alliance. Understanding these interests will help avoid unnecessary overlaps between the parties and potential competition between partners.

The mission of the collaboration needs to translate into a common vision of success for the alliance. All parties involved should have long-term goals in which the relationship plays a key role. The mission and vision for the collaboration must translate into a clear and appropriate set of objectives supported by each partner. Key stakeholders in the partner organizations outside the collaboration also should support the objectives.

With this in mind, the early meetings between the partners should allocate time to agree on the overall objectives of the alliance. They also should spend time establishing ground rules on how the parties will work together. My experience is that these early meetings need to be conducted face to face, if possible, as these issues are best discussed with all parties in the same room. The result of these early discussion should be convergence of purpose, a common vision of success, and motivation around short-term and long-term goals.

Identifying the Right Alliance Partner(s)

It is obvious, but not always apparent, that a successful collaboration starts with identifying the right partner with which to ally. Alliance partners must be competent in a desired area of expertise or have a technology that a partner needs. If the partners are not competent in an expertise or technology, there is little chance of success in the collaboration.

A clear foundation for a successful, innovative collaboration is a high degree of mutual respect and trust between partners. Even if partners have necessary expertise and resources, it is best to avoid partners with a reputation of skullduggery, conniving, deceit, and an attitude of winning at all costs. However, this sometimes cannot be avoided when equity or expertise is unique to that organization. A key strategy for success is to find a partner that brings the necessary skills, technologies, and equity to the partnership, who also has a reputation for collaborating well with others and has experience in forming successful collaborative relationships that are productive.

As a leader, you should develop the skills and reputation for forming collaborative relationships and being a partner of choice. When identifying the right partner(s) for an alliance, include a discussion around whether the partner has the resources and technologies to reach your strategic goals.

Potential Synergies in the Collaboration

For an alliance to be judged as successful, it must create synergies that make the alliance greater than the efforts of the individual partners. Potential synergies come from the partners' strengths and weaknesses complementing each other. Alliances between strong and weak companies rarely work. The alliance also should aim to bring together each partner's abilities to create new strengths.

Alliances work most efficiently if each partner is individually excellent and all partners are strong and have something to contribute to the alliance. Alliance partners must demonstrate interdependence and commit to work together to be successful. They cannot deliver on the work without their partners.

Driving to Outcome and Deliverables

Clearly, an alliance must yield benefit to all partners. Successful collaborations should yield benefits beyond the reasons for why partners enter the relationship and should offer the opportunity to create options to open new lines of research and new ideas. Parties should view collaborations as growth opportunities for all partners. Successful collaborations that endure can evolve beyond their initial expectations and objectives into new areas of innovation.

It is critical that alliances deliver visible achievement of benefit to the partners. An example of outcomes and deliverables is implementing a project plan to deliver an idea that will be used to investigate a new product. Clearly, if the alliance partners do not achieve this deliverable, the collaboration will not be viewed as a success.

Alliance Structure Planning and Governance

A successful collaboration needs to be well planned. Participants need to manage the start-up phase of the alliance with a deliberate implementation. Mutual investment in the collaboration needs to be clear and clearly articulated.

Each partner's organization needs to give the alliance a formal status within their organization. The alliance also should have a strong inter-firm coordination to serve as the foundation of the collaborative effort.

Typically, alliances create a new set of management practices and a new way of doing business. The alliance should have a clear governance structure including joint research committees, collaborative teams, and an escalation process to resolve issues. The governance structure should provide clear authority and guidelines for decision-making and conflict resolution.

A good case of where collaborations can create a new set of practices involves taking the best practices from each partner for governance systems, milestone tracking, or project management. My experience is that it is possible to learn from different organizations' ways of approaching these issues and subsequently changing their own internal process. How decisions are made within and outside of the alliance need to be clear and transparent.

The governance system also helps the alliance grow and adapt the scope based on success. This requires that the alliance governance structure ensures flexibility so the partners can be nimble and agile in addressing new opportunities.

Trust and Relationship Factors

Successful alliances manage the relationship, not just the deal. In leading collaborations, the leader needs to consider how the alliance will build trust and relationships within the alliance. Relationship-based elements include organization cultures, chemistry between partners, working together to collaborate, leadership, communication, and building trust.

Organizational Differences

The success of an innovative collaboration depends on the ability to identify and manage cultural differences such as inter-organizational differences and the differences between large and small companies. As already pointed out, cultural differences can be a major barrier to innovation.

Issues may include compatibility, philosophy, strategic objectives, common experiences, and organizational values and principles. It is difficult to manage differences in these aspects, so transparency and understanding of position are important communication requirements. It is also important to have a degree of integration and develop linkages and shared ways of operating smoothly within the alliance.

National cultural differences can complicate organizational culture differences when collaborators are international in nature. Face-to-face interactions are desirable but may not be possible. In the early stages of the alliance, the parties should establish clear ground rules on how to communicate.

Another management tool that can help establish understanding is for partners to articulate how organizational policies work within their companies, how they make decisions, and who needs to buy in to decisions. They also need to articulate how they will measure alliance success including clear milestones and how they will be judged on collaboration. One role of a leader in this type of alliance is to identify and manage cultural differences between partners.

Chemistry Between Alliance Partners

Effective collaborations depend on building chemistry between partners and the ability to cooperate efficiently. Positive chemistry results from positive team-oriented, trust-filled relationships. Obviously, it also comes from the success of the collaboration. One could argue that a company cannot have good external harmony unless it achieves it internally. Internal alignment is important in clear communications.

Managing partners' chemistry starts in the early stages of the alliance. It is important for the key individuals who will collaborate to get to know each other. They need to take time for building the relationship. Again, this is best achieved through face-to-face interactions.

Working Together to Collaborate

Creating an environment where people can share ideas and build upon them enhances collaboration and innovation. Good teamwork is important and depends on many factors (see Chapter 9). One of the most essential factors is the stability of personnel. It is important to keep the right participants involved in the alliance for the duration of the collaboration.

Creating stability depends heavily on creating harmony among alliance members. This harmony is not a peaceful relaxing bliss; rather, it is harmonious tension that leads to pushing the team to take risk and think out of the box. Positive team behaviors are needed for alliances to be innovative and collaborative, and those behaviors include transcending individual interests for the good of the team.

Alliance Leadership

An essential factor in alliance is the commitment and support of leadership. Often, it is a challenge to get consistency of position within large firms with changing priorities. In successful collaborations, once the alliance commences, responsibility for success shifts from the strategists, dealmakers, and top executives to champions and an implementation team of alliance managers and scientists.

The alliance needs explicitly structured governance bodies for decision-making and issue resolution. These bodies should consider partners as equals, subscribe to management by consensus, and not resort to dominance.

An important point to consider here is time for management attention. One of the scarcest resources in large organizations is the time that management can dedicate to any part of their often-large workload. Every collaboration partner, no matter how large or small, expects senior management to pay attention to it. Small companies expect senior staff from large companies to attend meetings. This can cause some significant scheduling issues due to limited management attention time.

A good indicator of effective alliance leadership is the extent to which the collaboration partners are empowered to make decisions. For instance, in a pharmaceutical company, scientists should be allowed to make decisions on how to proceed with innovative science without the burden of needing to involve senior management from either of the partners in the collaboration.

Communication and Technology

Effective communication is one of the most obvious and important success factors in alliances. However, it is often one of the most difficult to get right. Communication structures should be simple and should overcome genuine difficulties for managers. The alliance communication structure should minimize imperfect information, uncertain situations, and assessments. Information should be exchanged in a reasonable open manner within the legal structure defined in the agreement.

An example of effective communication includes the use of shared electronic tools such as e-rooms. Participants can use such tools to share and organize information in a version-controlled environment. This allows for open communication and sharing information, and it minimizes the chances of miscommunications or participants not sharing communications with everyone involved in the alliance.

Assessing Partnering Effectiveness in Alliances

In addition to the ten factors described above, my original research and follow-up study revealed some important points to consider as a leader involved in collaborations. Leaders can assess any alliance according to the four dimensions in Figure 3.

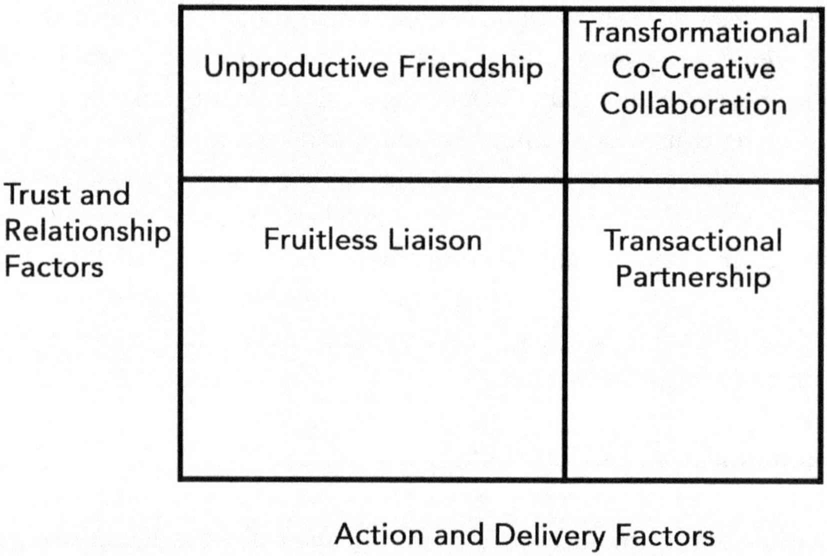

Trust and Relationship Factors	Unproductive Friendship	Transformational Co-Creative Collaboration
	Fruitless Liaison	Transactional Partnership

Action and Delivery Factors

Figure 3 – Framework for Assessing Effectiveness of Collaborative Alliances.

What are the characteristics of each dimension in the framework?

Fruitless Liaison: If the collaboration is low on trust and delivery, the collaboration will not deliver on its purpose, and there will be a lack of trust between the parties that could result in lack of innovation and co-creative activities.

Unproductive Friendship: If the collaboration is high on trust and relationship but low on task and delivery, it is probably a nice collaboration to be part of, but it does not deliver on its purpose.

Transactional Partnership: If the collaboration is high on task and delivery but low on trust and relationship, it probably delivers on the basic activities but will not go beyond that to deliver innovative solutions. The partners probably play it safe and are not willing to take the risk needed to be truly creative.

For example, if you work with a service provider for a single or a few transactions, the level of trust does not need to be high other than trusting the provider to deliver the promised quality of work on time. If you work with a plumber to fix a leaking pipe, you may not need a high level of relationship or trust beyond that needed to fix the leak.

Transformational Co-creative Collaboration: These are collaborations that deliver on their tasks but also can be co-creative and innovative because the parties trust each other and are willing to work together on high-risk ideas. In most collaborations, alliances need to strive to be in this part of the grid.

For a collaboration to be co-creative and deliver work that is more than just a routine service and is viewed as transformational work, it needs to be high on relationship and trust and high on task delivery factors.

CHARLES S. DORMER

Energizing, Impactful Leadership in Action: Building a Transformational Alliance

When Henry graduated with his medical degree, he had little idea of how exciting his career would be. He had a passion for clinical research, and he obtained his PhD researching new biomarkers to detect Parkinson's disease. He had a passion for helping patients and realized the best way for him to impact patients' lives was to continue his research in a large pharmaceutical company.

During the first ten years of his career, Henry was not disappointed and contributed to the research and development of several potential new treatments for patients with neurological conditions. He also had the opportunity to demonstrate his leadership skills in his small team of researchers and in leading several projects that involved people from across the R&D organization.

He built a reputation in his organization as being a credible leader who could get things done. He was authentic in his actions and built trust with his peers, boss, and his team. He was known as being a "straight shooter" but also took the time to listen to everyone's opinions and ideas. Part of his credibility came from his knowledge of science; he published several peer-reviewed articles including one in *Nature Journal*. But his credibility also came from his executive presence and his leadership style.

One key to his success was his ability to collaborate with other scientists, and he successfully worked with others researching in his field who were academics at some of the top universities. These research collaborations yielded some exciting results, and they fueled interesting advances that could be applied to the research and development of his firm's drugs.

Henry also had a reputation for having a strategic mindset. He worked with several colleagues on a proposal to collaborate with several universities and health care companies to define research to identify new methods for clinical research. This was a big proposal and would require a major investment from his company. Negotiations occurred with the universities and health care companies over the past year, and the legal complexity of this deal was immense.

If this collaboration were successful, Henry knew it could advance the field of biomarkers in several diseases and help his firm's drug-discovery efforts. The negotiations with the outside entities were not easy, and he still had doubts as to whether they would ever come to an agreement.

One evening, Henry received a text message from his boss, Emily: "Henry, I just got into town. We need to talk about the academic proposal. Let's meet in your office tomorrow morning at 8:00." Henry had a sinking feeling and thought the deal must be off. Why else would Emily be in town and want to see him?

At the meeting the next morning, Emily explained that she heard from the CEO of the company and company lawyers, and all parties signed the agreement. The deal was a go.

They would establish a steering committee at the most senior level, and she would sit on that committee. There also would be a science committee that would lead the research and allocate research funds to academics and other researchers in the collaboration. Emily asked Henry to lead that committee and lead the scientific efforts for the company. In effect, he would lead the real work of the collaboration: the science. Henry immediately agreed, and they agreed to discuss plans further in the weeks to come.

After Emily left, Henry pondered this huge opportunity. It would be a huge challenge for Henry, and he knew a lot was riding on this collaboration being successful. He knew success would depend on the collaboration going beyond just having good management of the alliance; the different parties would need to collaborate to create new science together. As was his nature, the excitement of the opportunity overcame the doubts and the challenges he saw. But where to start? What did Henry need to do to be a collaborative leader to make this venture successful? How could he go beyond just managing the alliance to leading a co-creative network of this complexity?

He knew that the alliance would need to create a new organization that was independent of the partner organizations; so, he had to create a third entity. This new entity must balance the needs of all the partners, and he would need to keep the internal stakeholders in his company aligned to the purpose and strategic goals of the alliance. In some respects, he would need to be the leader of the alliance and the representative of his company.

The aim and purpose of this collaboration was clear: develop a world-leading network with excellence in biomarker discovery and development and have an impact on the discovery and development of new drugs and treatments. Through this collaboration, they could take advantage of the best academics in the field through the universities, experience in drug discovery and development of drugs through Henry's company, and access to patients for clinical trials through the health care companies.

Even though the benefits for each partner differed, there was an opportunity for all the partners to advance their agendas. The academics would get funding for their research to advance the science and publish papers. Henry's company would help to develop new science that could be used in the clinical trials of its new drugs. The health care companies could help their patients and have an impact on the broader health of the community.

Henry started to consider some of the challenges he would need to overcome. Comprising the alliance were academic organizations and research organizations as well as his large pharmaceutical company. The different sizes and the nature of these organizations, their motivations, and their different agendas would be challenging to navigate. Henry knew that this collaboration would be as much a leadership challenge as a business or science challenge.

For the alliance to succeed, Henry was aware that he would need to lead the team to deliver on its tasks and build relationships among the partners that would build trust so that the alliance could be innovative and creative. He needed a plan to ensure that he could be a strategic leader in both these aspects.

Henry's first step was hiring a coach who could help him develop these leadership skills but also work with the collaboration to facilitate their interactions. The coach would give feedback to Henry and the collaboration partners in respect to the dynamics of how the partners worked together.

Henry organized a kickoff meeting of the alliance partners that would be the decision-makers for the science of the partnership. At that first meeting, the partners discussed the reasons that they entered the alliance, the vision and purpose of the collaboration; their individual strengths and potential synergies, the structure of decision-making, and project management. They also discussed some ground rules for how they would work together to maximize building trustful relationships, ensuring they raised diverse ideas and that everyone would be included, making the most of their differences and not letting them become barriers to the alliance, how they would raise and resolve conflicts, how they would communicate and use technology, and how they would create a safe environment in the team to encourage innovation and creativity. Simply put, they discussed how they would create positive energy in the collaboration and minimize negative energy.

After the kickoff meeting, Henry and his coach reviewed the progress the team made in that first interaction. It was a two-day, face-to-face meeting. Henry worried that the investment of time and travel would be viewed as a big price to pay. After all, in that first meeting they barely started to talk about the science of the collaboration. But on reflection, it was clear that laying down the building blocks of the collaboration in that meeting proved to be critical.

During the meeting, participants raised many concerns, and they resolved some of the uncertainty there and then. The team also had a chance to get to know each other, which would make it easier to work together. They were off to a great start, but Henry knew this was the start of a journey and he would need to apply all his collaborative leadership skills and develop new ones for this alliance to be successful.

Henry knew his leadership of the collaboration would be of little value if it did not deliver results. He also needed to have a structure in place that would help to manage the individual projects. There needed to be a return on the investments that his science committee made, including managing resources and delivering on an agreed timeline.

The challenge for Henry was that the academic groups were not used to being managed in this way. Traditionally, most of the academics were used to receiving grants and conducted their science without much accountability for delivering on time and on budget. Henry's large pharmaceutical company was used to project-management and portfolio-management systems that could be bureaucratic and burdensome. Henry would need to manage this situation carefully to institute a system that would give a level of control of how the investments were managed without stifling the innovation required for this type of discovery science. Henry needed to develop an action plan for leading and managing the science committee and the portfolio of investments they made.

Henry worked with his partners in the collaboration to establish their science committee. He attracted top executives from the health care companies and senior academics from the universities to join his committee and established early success.

He worked with his coach and defined an action plan that included six goals. (1) Work on ensuring they were making the most of some partners' strengths to complement the weaknesses of other partners. (2) Be more effective in managing the research projects and be more open to new ideas. (3) Strengthen the inter-firm coordination and increase the number of projects involving multiple institutions. (4) Be open to learning from these different views and experiences; be more open and learn about the different organizations' culture and be more inclusive. (5) Update the contact lists and define clear roles and responsibilities within the collaboration and their parent organizations. (6) Improve the shared communication technologies to help minimize the sharing of imperfect information and to improve communication between scientists involved in the collaboration.

Over the next six months, Henry worked with his team to implement his plans. The team soon built trust in each other, and their relationships were open and honest. Henry celebrated the success of this group and, before long, the research started to pay off. They were able to publish several articles in peer-reviewed journals, and they developed several scientific assays that could be applied to clinical trials to test new drugs.

CHARLES S. DORMER

Chapter Summary

An important part of being an energizing, impactful leader delivering on strategy and purpose is accessing talent, resources, technology, and intellectual property through partnerships, alliances, and collaborations. This involves collaborating with many groups and individuals who are not under the leader's direct control.

It is not uncommon for leaders to lead complex networks of collaborators from different types of organizations that come together to solve a common problem. In these collaborations, there is a need to go beyond traditional alliance management to collaborative leadership, to lead transformational, co-creative networks of organizations.

There are many challenges with complex partnerships that may be due to the different size and nature of the partners and their organizations. Energizing, impactful leaders need to deal with challenges that come from differences in decision-making and organizational politics. They also must deal with challenges associated with the legal complexities of many partners working together. Organizations also may have differences in their motivations and may bring different agendas to the table. There also are challenges associated with the ability to manage conflict that may occur in the partnership and inside participating organizations. To be successful in the collaboration, the partnership must form a "third entity," separate and distinct from the organizations involved.

To be successful in this environment, energizing, impactful leaders need to be proficient in factors associated with task and delivery as well as trust and relationships.

Task and delivery factors include internal leadership skills such as strategic thinking, strategic goals, and system thinking. Success in collaborations requires identifying the right partners, maximizing potential synergies between partners, and driving outcomes and deliverables. The alliance structure should include a governance structure for decision-making.

Trust and relational factors require that the leader have a high degree of self-awareness, empathy, and authenticity. The leader needs to create an environment in the collaboration that includes all collaboration partners. Complex partnerships with many partners give a leader an opportunity to have many different views and ideas surfacing from different organizational, professional, and national cultures. Leaders should take advantage of these cultural differences and the chemistry between the partners.

The complexities of leading an alliance with external partners requires that a leader build trust and relationships with stakeholders both inside and outside the partnership in the partner's organization.

To succeed in managing collaborative alliances, leaders need to develop skills that enable the following efforts. (1) Clearly define and communicate a strategy, purpose, and vision for the alliance. (2) Assess and select a partner with the right technical expertise, resources, and experience. (3) Recognize the technical strengths of partners and how they complement each other and are aligned. (4) Have the ability to drive outcomes going beyond the agreement, which benefit partners with growth opportunities.

Energetic, impactful leaders also need to possess conflict management and project skills. They must build trust in the alliance through influencing skills and courageous leadership (team and stakeholders). To be successful, they also must create the optimal culture within the alliance by understanding and appreciating cultural differences and diversity. They form a team and manage the team dynamics to learn from successes and failures, share ideas, and be creative. Finally, they manage communication and collaboration technologies to ensure clarity and understanding and overcome challenges associated with being virtual.

Key Learnings for Leading Collaborative Alliances

- Energizing, impactful leaders collaborate with others through internal and external alliances.
- They recognize that delivering their purpose, vision, and strategic goals is not just a genius endeavor but also requires that they engage with people and groups outside their formal control and inspire them toward common goals.
- They overcome the challenges that come with complex networks of organizations working together.
- They build and manage relationships and trust.
- They also manage and track actions needed to deliver strategic goals and objectives.

Action Plan for Improving Capability to Lead in Collaborative Alliances

In your action plan, take time to reflect on your strengths and your opportunity for growth. This self-reflection has two parts. First, review the following questions and rate yourself for a strength or an opportunity for growth for each question. Next, think about actions that you can take to enhance your strength or develop your opportunity for growth.

1. Can you clearly define and communicate a strategy, purpose, and vision for the alliance?
2. Can you assess and select a partner with the right technical expertise, resources, and experience?
3. What is your ability to recognize the technical strengths of partners and how they complement each other and are aligned?
4. What is your ability to drive outcomes going beyond the agreement that will benefit partners with growth opportunities?
5. Can you manage the alliance (conflict management, project, and alliance management)?
6. What is your ability to build trust in partnering through your influencing skills and courageous leadership?
7. What is your ability to create the optimal culture within an alliance by understanding and appreciating cultural differences and diversity?
8. Can you manage team dynamics and create a positive environment?
9. Can you create an alliance that learns from successes and failures, shares ideas, and is creative?
10. Can you manage communication and collaborative technologies to ensure clarity and understanding?

Chapter 11
Creating Energy to Drive Change: Delivering as an Energizing, Impactful Leader

Way back in Chapter 1, you first learned of the Integrated Framework for Energizing, Impactful Leadership. Each subsequent chapter focused on various elements in that framework. This final chapter shows you how to draw together all the elements and integrate them into a single approach that you can take to become a highly effective leader (indeed, an energizing, impactful leader).

But, first, let us look at the context for your leadership experiences, because leaders today face unprecedented challenges and opportunities. And you will need to lead through change associated with both.

At the time of writing this book, the world is in the middle of a crisis and beginning of a worldwide economic recession due to the COVID-19 pandemic. At this time, no one knows how long it will last. Company leaders now need to figure out how to preserve cash but at the same time invest in technologies that will position them to be competitive. The forced shutdowns of business worldwide during the crisis resulted in many people working remotely from home. Leaders must understand how this work-from-home model changes the dynamics of how people work.

Leaders now need to manage complex virtual networks of employees. They need to make decisions on how to monitor performance and drive increased productivity in this new model. They also need to decide whether they want to keep all their facilities or sell some. Should they even divest some business units? And they need to make decisions on what products and services to retain or discard because the pandemic also impacted people's buying habits and changed their expectations.

Other challenges emerged before the pandemic. People now stay in the workforce for a longer period. Leaders now must deal with diverse generational expectations and skills differing among baby boomers, generation X and Y, and millennials. Leaders must try to create harmony among their differing expectations, mindsets, and motivations.

The pace of change and technology development is now much faster. And entire industries are disrupted by new competitors using new technology and digital business models. Changing the status quo when employees want to resist change becomes even more difficult at today's pace of change.

Leaders need to create energy in followers now more than ever before to achieve strategic goals in this rapidly changing environment. At the same time, leaders must help their followers (and themselves) deal with conditions that are more volatile, uncertain, complex, and ambiguous (VUCA) than in the past. Emotions arising from these conditions can hinder achieving strategic goals.

Advances in technology and education deliver great opportunities to solve problems that in the past seemed unsolvable. And technology gives leaders access to people's ideas, experiences, and skills from across the world so they can leverage them in solving problems and achieving strategic goals. But leaders must create positive environments that enable employees to collaborate and take action together to achieve goals.

If you use the Integrated Framework for Energizing, Impactful Leadership I recommend in this book, you will gain the capabilities to deal with this evolving complex world. Recall, for instance, how the leaders in the action plan examples in this book strived to have a big impact in the world.

Mary worked to find cures for cancer, a disease that is still a major cause of death throughout the world. Greg and Sari sought treatments for rare diseases with an unmet medical need. Anne and Megan worked across disciplines in science to help patients with untreatable diseases. Mo brought IT solutions to complex problems. Philippe and his team focused on finding ways of manufacturing antibodies to treat inflammatory diseases. Naomi worked to produce medical devices that could improve the quality of life for patients. Finally, Henry worked with external collaborators to find methods that could detect earlier the onset of disease.

I took most examples in this book from the health care field. But now, more than ever, we need great leaders to step up and effectively lead to solve big problems and implement change. Think, for instance, of your organization's leadership succeeding in solving problems in such areas as climate change, world populations and demographics, mental health, racial injustice, aging populations, and addiction.

Each leader in the examples in this book had a clear and compelling vision that would impact the world. They recognized that gone are the days when a single "genius" can deliver a solution to a problem; so, they knew they would need to build groups of followers who go would beyond average performance levels to deliver their vision. You will need to do that, too. They needed other people around them to align around their strategy and be willing to follow and to be engaged. To achieve this, they needed to create positive energy in their teams and collaborators through their leadership. This energy could not be just short bursts; it had to be created in a way that would be sustained. They were in a marathon, not a sprint. All the leaders in this book managed energy dynamics through their leadership skills. You will need to do that, too.

They also knew that the outcome measure of their leadership would be whether they delivered on the strategic goals and actions for their area of responsibility. There are several outcome metrics that any leader may use to assess their delivery of actions; the metrics depend on the nature of their work.

For example, for a CEO of a public company, outcome metrics would be profit and loss and stock price. For a leader of a construction project, it may be delivering on time, on budget, and to an agreed level of quality. For a scientist, it may be scientific papers or experimental data. For a product development leader, it may be delivering a new product to market or achieving a new level of innovation. Delivering on actions requires operational excellence and uses management systems.

Ultimately, you (like the leaders in stories in this book) cannot succeed in your leadership endeavors unless you deliver on your strategic goals. The good news is you now have all the information and insights you need if you follow the Integrated Framework for Energizing, Impactful Leaders.

Energizing, Impactful Leadership

Never forget that one of the most important roles of a leader is to create and manage energy to drive change. Energizing, impactful leaders understand how energy works in their organizations, and they know how to create positive energy and minimize the impact of negative energy. This organizational energy is critical to align people in an organization to deliver a desired vision and strategy. Great leaders understand the dynamics around energy creation and how to effectively manage that energy.

The key measure for assessing the impact of your leadership is the level of energy you generate and manage with the people with whom you work. To illustrate this point, let us consider the example of Winston Churchill's leadership.

Most people agree that Winston Churchill was a great leader during World War II. Historians recount that Britain was in a grave situation on May 28, 1940. Churchill had been Prime Minister for less than three weeks, and his key cabinet members wrestled on that day with the question of whether Britain should join the fight in the war. Churchill's advisors were divided on this question and in a stalemate situation. Historians also documented how Churchill appealed to the emotions of British people and convinced his cabinet not to pursue surrender. We now know, of course, that the decision of that group, influenced by Churchill's speech before the cabinet, changed the course of history.

I am not a historian, but I can recognize the great leadership Churchill showed in that event. He created energy around his vision to resist Nazi Germany and not to appease Adolf Hitler. Initially, he created that energy with his cabinet and the British Parliament. He went on to create energy in the British people. The energy he created aligned the country to fight and resist, even in the face of great hardship and sacrifice that followed his decision.

Obviously, most of us in a business context do not lead in a situation that requires our team to make those kinds of sacrifices, but the principle holds true. The role of a leader is to create and manage energy to make bold decisions, take bold actions, and inspire a group of followers to achieve great things. I included a quote in an inspiring speech by Churchill at the beginning of the Introduction to this book.

What about the impact Churchill made? History would remember his actions very differently if he did not ultimately motivate Britain to win the war. Creating energy was not a one-time event for Churchill. He sustained the commitment to resist through the dark times of the "Blitz." To achieve his strategic goals in the long term, he continued to build energy through his leadership style.

Ultimately, the outcome measure of his leadership was that he delivered on the strategic goals and tasks that resulted in the defeat of Hitler in 1945. Churchill was an energizing, impactful leader in the fact that he created positive energy and delivered on his strategic goals.

Outcomes of Leaders Not Creating Energy

Figure 4 shows the relationship between the energy created by leaders and delivering actions and strategic goals.

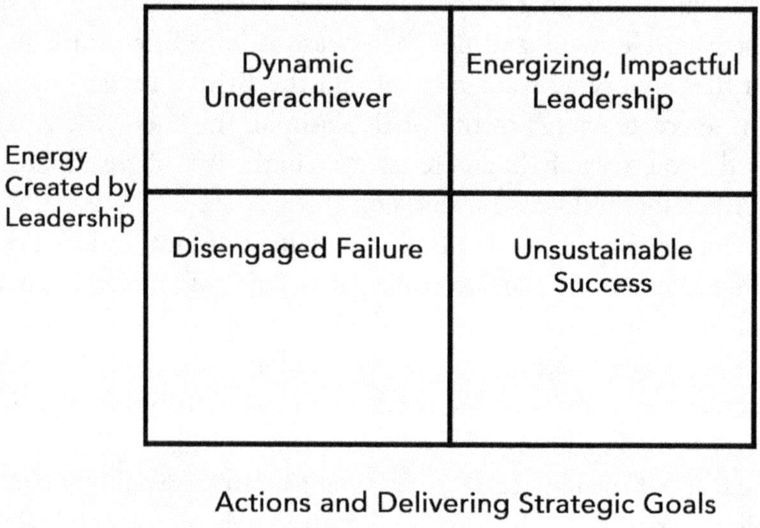

Energy Created by Leadership	Dynamic Underachiever	Energizing, Impactful Leadership
	Disengaged Failure	Unsustainable Success

Actions and Delivering Strategic Goals

Figure 4 – Energizing, Impactful Leadership

Interpreting the diagram in Figure 4, if a leader fails to create energy in an organization and it does not deliver on the tasks or strategic goals, the group can be described as a "disengaged failure." If an organization delivers but is low in energy, the organization may deliver in the short term, but there is a risk that people are disengaged, and the top talent may leave. I describe this as "unsustainable success." If the organization is high on energy created by a leader but does not deliver on goals, this is a "dynamic underachievement" organization.

The aim of strategic leadership is to be high on energy and high on delivery. This is "energizing, impactful leadership." Figure 4 is a tool for assessing where an organization is today and where it needs to be.

I worked in some organizations that seemed to fluctuate between dynamic underachievement and unsustainable success. They were either a high-energy organization that fell short of delivering their potential or were driven by short-term goals that caused people to experience burnout. Achieving energizing, impactful leadership involves building energy, engagement, motivation, and delivering on short-term and long-term goals.

Journey to Becoming an Energizing, Impactful Leader

In the Foreword and Introduction, I explained that your process of learning how to become an energizing, impactful leader is a journey. This book is your road map for that journey.

The Integrated Framework for Energizing, Impactful Leadership (shown in Figure 1 in Chapter 1 and displayed here again as Figure 5) incorporates two elements that relate to creating energy by leadership: developing self-wisdom through self-reflection and signaling to others in a way that influences other and builds effective relationships. The other two elements in the framework relate to actions and delivering strategic goals: defining strategies and goals in the context of their purpose and system and understanding and implementing actions.

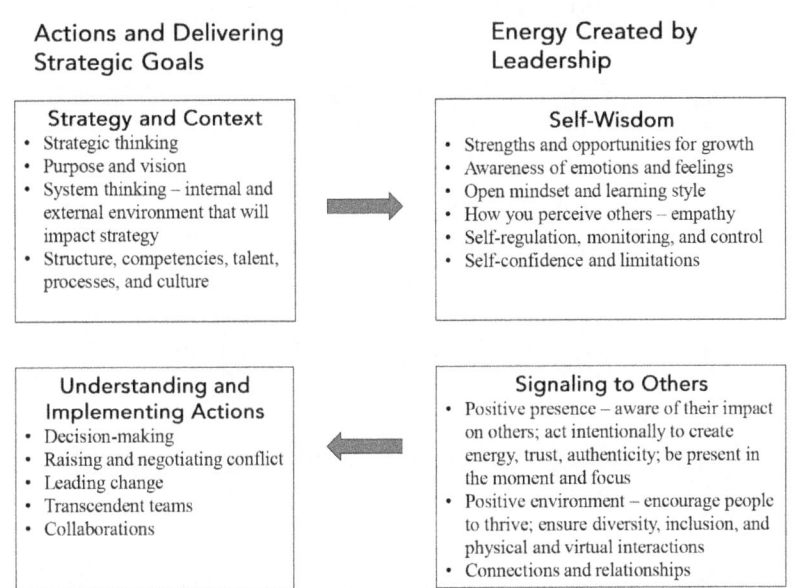

Figure 5 - Integrated Framework for Energizing, Impactful Leaders

As you become an energizing, impactful leader, you will develop strength in all four elements. In other words, you will be clear about your strategic goals in the context of your purpose and system. You will have a high degree of self-wisdom. You will signal to others in a way that builds energy in others and builds effective relationships. You will take action to deliver your strategies.

It is not possible to be an effective leader if you lack one of the four elements. For example, if you do not build a clear strategy within the context of your system, it becomes difficult to inspire others to follow. If you lack a strong degree of self-wisdom, you risk others perceiving you as unauthentic or unpredictable. If you are not effective at building relationships and influencing others, you risk being alone in your mission or having to spend time trying to overcome your followers' resistance to your strategy. Finally, if you are not effective at taking actions, you risk failing to deliver on your strategy. Lack of any of the four elements in the integrated framework may lead to your being derailed and failing to be successful.

Integrating Key Learnings on How to Become an Energizing, Impactful Leader

Let us now integrate the Key Learnings presented at the end of Chapters 2-10 with the actions you need to take as an energizing, impactful leader. The outline below segments the learnings from each chapter and actions according to the four elements illustrated in the integrated framework. As the integrated framework diagram shows, each element builds upon the other elements and results in an effective flow.

Element #1: Strategy in Context

Action: Define strategies and goals in the context of purpose and system.
Leadership Topic: Strategy and context
- Strategic thinking
- Purpose and vision

- System thinking
- Structure, competencies, talent, processes, and culture

Key Learnings From Chapter 2

- Energizing, impactful leaders are strategic thinkers, as they know their purpose that drives them and creates energy.
- They have clear and powerful strategic goals that focus their energy and inspire others to follow.
- Their purpose evokes an emotional response in themselves and others.
- They are analytical in identifying their goals; they understand opportunities and challenges opportunities in their internal and external environments that will impact their strategy.

Key Learnings From Chapter 3

- Energizing, impactful leaders are system thinkers. They analyze the system in which they are a part, and they frame their strategic plans and actions in the context of the whole system, not individual parts.
- They understand their internal organization including structure, competencies, talent, processes, and culture.
- They understand their external environments and recognize patterns, trends, challenges, interconnections, and interactions with their system.
- They analyze the gap between their current state and a desired future state that is needed to deliver their strategic goals.

Element #2: Self-Wisdom

Action: Develop self-wisdom through self-reflection.
Leadership Topic: Self-wisdom
- Strengths and opportunities for growth

- Awareness of emotions and feelings (triggers)
- Open mindset and learning style
- How you perceive others (empathy)
- Self-regulation, monitoring, and control
- Self-confidence and knowing limitations

Key Learnings From Chapter 4

- Energizing, impactful leaders are self-aware, empathetic, and have an open mindset. They know their strengths and weaknesses. Importantly, they can identify their emotions and feelings.
- They have a high level of self-control. They focus on their goals and not becoming distracted.
- They are self-confident and recognize their limitations.
- They are empathetic to others. They seek to understand other people's perspectives. They empathize with what others feel and have a good sense of what others need.
- They have an open mindset. This mindset leads to a desire to learn and learn from criticism, embracing challenges, and having a greater sense of free will.

Element #3: Signaling to Others

Action: Signal to others in a way that builds energy and effective relationships.
Leadership Topic: Signaling to others
- Positive presence (awareness of impact on others, act intentionally to create energy and trust, authenticity, presence in the moment, and focus)
- Positive environment (encourage people to thrive; ensure diversity, inclusion, and physical and virtual interactions)
- Connections and relationships

Key Learnings From Chapter 5

- Energizing, impactful leaders influence others to follow their purpose and strategic goals by being aware and managing their positive presence.
- They are aware of the impact of their behavior on others. They intentionally act, communicate, and listen in ways that show a positive impact on others.
- They build and manage trust in their relationships.
- They are authentic (attuned to their most sincere selves, even under stress).
- They are present in the moment.

Key Learnings From Chapter 6

- Energizing, impactful leaders create a positive environment that encourages people to work toward the desired strategic impact and thrive and develop their talent.
- They take advantage of diversity and inclusion to facilitate creativity and innovation to deliver an organization's purpose and strategic goals.
- They create circumstances and conditions that generate positive energy, whether the workforce group is in the same office or works remotely.
- They create an environment where people feel the positive energy in everything they do and want to be part of it.

Element #4: Understanding and Implementing Actions

Action: Ensure your actions and implementation of your decisions are effective in enabling achieving your strategic goals.
Leadership Topic: Understanding and implementing actions
- Decision-making
- Raising and negotiating conflict

- Leading change
- Transcendent teams
- Collaborations

Key Learnings From Chapter 7

- Energizing, impactful leaders are effective in making decisions.
- They use a robust decision-making process that balances speed with rigor, involves the right people, and balances analysis while avoiding negative impacts of emotions and biases.
- Decision-making requires that a leader has a high degree of self-awareness and, if a group of people is involved, a high degree of group awareness.
- This process should result in an implementable and measurable course of action that leads to desired consequences.
- They also have courage of their convictions and follow through on their actions.

Key Learnings From Chapter 8

- Energizing, impactful leaders regard conflict as a positive way of thinking and source of creativity.
- They create an environment where people are not afraid to raise issues because it may cause conflict.
- They create an environment to encourage conflict resolution that separates positions from interests.
- They use negotiation skills to reach agreements that are mutually beneficial and aligned with purpose and goals.
- They separate substance from relationships.
- They invent options for mutual gain and use objective criteria to resolve conflict.
- Energizing, impactful leaders are effective at leading change.
- They know how to lead change to deliver on their vision and strategy.

- They follow a process for managing change that includes defining a vision. They understand their current system and future-state gaps, define change roles and responsibilities, develop action plans, manage implementation including short-term wins, measure, and monitor change, and build new approaches into business as usual.

Key Learnings From Chapter 9

- Energizing, impactful leaders build transcendent teams by managing styles, roles, and team dynamics.
- They pull together the right team composed of complementary skills, who commit to a common purpose, sense of urgency, performance goals, and approach.
- They form and manage effective teams that are diverse and take advantage of that diversity.
- They identify different styles and recognize that all are important for an effective team. They make the most of the different styles.
- They develop teams through all phases, beginning with formation through developing high performance and delivering the desired goal. They are aware of which phase the team is in and facilitate the team getting to the next level.
- They understand the challenges when teams are virtual. They leverage virtual distances and avoid common pitfalls that inhibit performance due to virtual team dynamics.

Key Learnings From Chapter 10

- Energizing, impactful leaders collaborate with others through internal and external alliances.
- They recognize that delivering their purpose, vision, and strategic goals is not just a genius endeavor but also requires that leaders engage with people and groups outside their formal control and inspire them toward achieving common goals.

- They overcome the challenges that come with complex networks of organizations working together.
- They build and manage relationships and trust.
- They also manage and track actions needed to deliver strategic goals and objectives.

Summarizing Your Leadership Impact

You create energy in others by having a clear purpose and meaningful vision that connects emotionally, and you communicate it to inspire others to follow with passion and engagement. You have a high level of focus and do not let setbacks distract you. By focusing on delivering purpose, you create positive energy.

You also have a personal positive presence that creates positive energy in others. You can generate positive energy in others if you demonstrate that you are sensitive to others' feelings, know what they need, and understand their perspectives (being empathetic). You are present in the moment for someone and not distracted by the past or worrying about future things that are out of your control.

You are willing to learn and grow, be open to feedback, and create a feeling of moving forward to something greater. You are intentional about forming positive relationships. Positive energy comes from leaders who are authentic and can be trusted, and who trust others. You are open to listening to others' perspectives and ideas, and positive energy comes from taking advantage of their diverse set of experiences and viewpoints and ensuring you include everyone.

Finally, you create a positive environment by helping others develop and thrive. Leaders generate positive energy when people feel that the leader cares about them and is interested in helping them to thrive and develop their careers.

You deliver on your strategic goals by having a robust decision-making process that avoids negative effects of biases and emotions. Energy comes from decisions that are transparent and perceived as fair. You also are open to people raising conflict and resolving conflict based on interests rather than positions.

Finally, you deliver goals by leading change and by following a change process. And you can deliver goals by creating transcendent teams and effective collaborations.

Simplify Your Journey to Becoming an Energizing, Impactful Leader

In my experience, the best way to undertake a complex journey is to first develop a plan. The same is true of your journey to become an energizing, impactful leader. The journey requires that you take time to reflect on your strengths and opportunities for growth as a strategic leader, and you need to build time for this effort into your plan.

Your Journey Plan

Start with Self-Reflection

To aid you in this necessary self-reflection, you should plan to review the list of action-plan self-assessment questions that appear at the end of each chapter of this book and think about how you rate yourself in those aspects either as a strength or as an opportunity for growth. Also, as you answer the questions, think of an example of when you demonstrated the strength and think of a situation when you could have done a better job.

The second part of your self-reflection is thinking about actions that you can take to enhance your strength or develop your opportunity for growth. In my experience, the more specific you can be in identifying these actions, the better chance you have of achieving that goal.

Visualize Success

Also, as part of this process, try to visualize what success will look like if you develop your strength further or take the opportunity for growth. Again, try to be specific and think about a business outcome you tried to achieve. There is a set of questions provided below to capture your thoughts.

Focus on Opportunities for Personal Growth

An example of an opportunity for growth may be that you do not focus your time on your real purpose. You find yourself not saying no to endless meetings that do not further your mission. An action plan to develop this opportunity may include improving your time-management skills and not reacting to every invitation to a meeting. You may set a goal that within three months you will focus only on meetings causally linked to your purpose. If you succeed in achieving this goal, the outcome is that you will enhance your focus on your purpose and see an increase in productivity.

Focus on Your Strengths

Remember to focus not only on development needs but also on strengths that you could further develop. By focusing on the areas that will have the biggest impact for you as a leader, you should get a good return on investment and involvement.

Reflect on Your Effectiveness

An approach to measuring your effectiveness is to take time reflecting on your efforts as an energizing, impactful leader. Effective leaders periodically reflect on their leadership impact. Advice in books, articles, and videos of dozens of leadership coaches suggests asking whether you made the best effort to achieve a goal rather than just asking if you achieved them. Using this approach, you can ask yourself the questions below regarding whether you made your best effort to be a strategic leader and behave in a way that generates energy in your organization.

Self- Reflection Questions Measuring Your Effectiveness

Did I try my best to ...
1. Inspire enthusiasm, passion, and energy in others?
2. Think about the external environment and competition and identify opportunities and challenges that will impact my strategy?
3. Demonstrate that I am self-aware (know my strengths and weaknesses) and know my expertise and limitations? (Am I in touch with how I feel at any given time and with the emotions I feel?)
4. Demonstrate a high degree of focus? (Do I pursue goals without distractions?)
5. Demonstrate that I understand other people's perspectives, pick up on how others feel, and have a good sense of what others need rather than just what they want?
6. Be open to learning from successes, frame failure as an opportunity to learn, and seek feedback from others and act upon it?
7. Listen effectively and communicate intentionally so that my nonverbal and verbal messages are consistent?
8. Develop an intentional plan to create a diverse and inclusive environment?
9. Have a robust process for making decisions (right people, right time, right analysis, and right options)?
10. See conflict as a way of thinking that is important to creativity and manage conflict that brings agreement to substance issues and preserves relationships?

Bottom line: If you execute your plan to develop the four integrated competencies (define strategy in context, acquire self-wisdom, signal to influence others and build relationships, and take action), you can become an energizing, impactful leader. By creating energy and managing dynamics through leadership and delivering strategic goals and actions, you can impact the world.

Becoming an energizing, impactful leader is a life-long journey. Do not forget to enjoy the scenery on your journey and do not be afraid to ask for directions if you get lost. Enjoy impacting the world in a positive way!

About the Author

Charles S. Dormer is a coach and teacher helping people at all levels maximize the speed of their journey to become energizing, impactful leaders.

Following a career of over thirty years working for some of the top global pharmaceutical companies (SmithKline Beecham, GlaxoSmithKline, Wyeth, Pfizer, and AstraZeneca), he embarked on a journey to help leaders.

He focuses on working with leaders to identify astute insights and leverages his broad experience to bring context to leadership behavior discussions. He specializes in leadership behaviors that energize others to follow and deliver strategic goals. In his work, he takes a results and action-oriented approach that cuts to the chase and gets to the heart of the matter by asking probing questions and testing assumptions. He uses systems thinking to organize issues into themes to help understand problems and implement solutions. Charles aims to have a significant impact on leaders' performance and help them address difficult, complex, business challenges.

Charles is also passionate about sharing his learning and experience through teaching and mentoring. He is the recipient of the "Excellence in Teaching Award – MS Biotechnology Program, Georgetown University. He holds an Adjunct Lecturer position at Georgetown University, where he directs a Program on Strategic Leadership in Science and Technology in the MS Biotechnology Course. Charles holds Master of Science (Honors) and Master of Philosophy degrees in Organizational Dynamics from the University of Pennsylvania.

Although originally from the United Kingdom, he moved to the United States over thirty years ago. He now lives in Bethany Beach, Delaware.

For further information or inquires regarding in-person or video-based consulting services, contact Charles Dormer at apexenergizingimpact@gmail.com. You can learn more about him at https://www.apexstp.com/.

www.ingramcontent.com/pod-product-compliance
Lightning Source LLC
Chambersburg PA
CBHW060107230426
43661CB00033B/1425/J